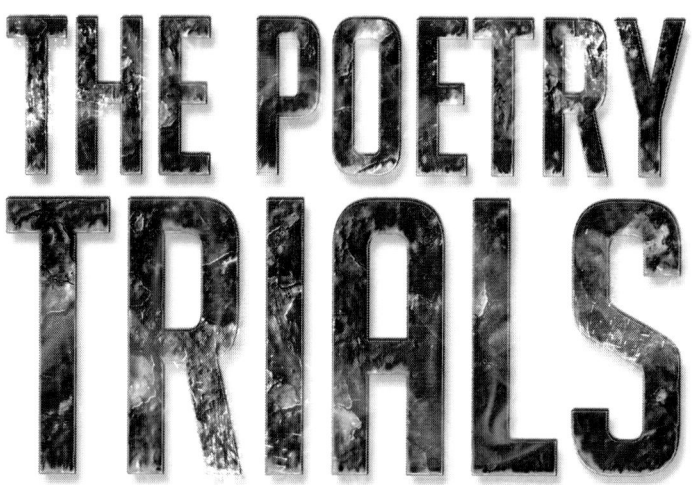

LONDON AND MIDDLESEX

Edited by Emily Wilson

First published in Great Britain in 2016 by:

Remus House
Coltsfoot Drive
Peterborough
PE2 9BF
Telephone: 01733 890066
Website: www.youngwriters.co.uk

All Rights Reserved
Book Design by Ashley Janson
© Copyright Contributors 2016
SB ISBN 978-1-78624-258-9
Printed and bound in the UK by BookPrintingUK
Website: www.bookprintinguk.com

FOREWORD

Welcome, Reader!

For Young Writers' latest competition, *The Poetry Trials*, we gave secondary school students nationwide the challenge of writing a poem. They were given the option of choosing a restrictive poetic technique, or to choose any poetic style of their choice. They rose to the challenge magnificently, with young writers up and down the country displaying their poetic flair.

We chose poems for publication based on style, expression, imagination and technical skill. The result is this entertaining collection full of diverse and imaginative poetry, which is also a delightful keepsake to look back on in years to come.

Here at Young Writers our aim is to encourage creativity in the next generation and to inspire a love of the written word, so it's great to get such an amazing response, with some absolutely fantastic poems. It made choosing the winners extremely difficult, so well done to *Ermer Stevens* who has been chosen as the best in this book. Their poem will go into a shortlist from which the top 5 poets will be selected to compete for the ultimate Poetry Trials prize.

I'd like to congratulate all the young poets in *The Poetry Trials - London And Middlesex* - I hope this inspires them to continue with their creative writing.

Jenni Bannister

Editorial Manager

CONTENTS

Kaosi Mbaeri (14) 1

Abbey Manor College, London
Paige Ricketts (14) 2
Miekella Grant-Irish (13) 3

Acton High School, London
Aiysha McInnes (13) 4
Rawan Badreddine (12) 4
Ella Torbett (12) 5
Kweku Isaiah James Anoom (12) 5
Najma Abdulkadir (13) 6
Evan Spencer (13) 7
Francesca Birri (13) 8
Baraa Sheryanna (12) 8
Caitlin May Wales (13) 9
Leon Gjata (13) 9
Aggie Bright (13) 10
Andre Arnaoudov (11) 11
Jaydon Goodfellow (12) 12
Emily Laura Page (11) 13
Ifrah Hussain (12) 14
Ella Edwards (12) 15
Hassan Edaan (12) 16
Jamal Mohamed (13) 17
Lamiah Persaud-Hibbert (12) 18
Somaya Damhoun (11) 18
Dawud Mazidi (12) 19
Zuzanna Rakowska (12) 20
Akram Kassim (13) 21
Shaniyah Blake Eccleston (11) 22
Joshua Carr (11) 23
Alfred Davis (12) 24
Matthew Smart (11) 24
Kasem Oakley (16) 25
Mohamed Ali (13) 26
Kayla Hughes (11) 27
Sergio Srowronski (12) 28
Nilkanth Kalan (11) 29

Deptford Green School, London
Taiyyabah Khan (13) 29
Anastacia Mary Koncz (15) 30
Michele Cascella (15) 30
Princess Dumenu (15) 31
Adelina Ajrizaj (15) 32
Kareem Harris (15) 33
Denise Victoria Lawrence (11) 34
Josh Heloussala (15) 35
Bailey Peden (15) 36
Kieran Appleby (14) 36

Forest Hill School, London
James Casey (12) 37
Nana Boahene (12) 38
Jack Morrish (13) 38
Travis Burchell (14) 39
Kewen Wang (12) 40
Marc Morgan (11) 41

Harris City Academy Crystal Palace, London
Kang Mbang (12) 42
Katerina Kennedy (12) 43
Anika Collins (11) 44
Kirsti Jones (11) 45
Jamiliah Oppong (11) 46
Ita Hermine Neumeyer (12) 47
Riaz Pathan (12) 48
Jamilah Alisha Williams (12) 49
Zoe Donkor (12) 49
Theo Chapman (12) 50
Rosanne Choong (12) 51
Daniel May (13) 52
Humzah Mohomed (13) 53
Jai Sood (13) 54
Ulrich Petri-Dawes (11) 55
Zaina-Rene Hannah Francis (11) 56

Highgate Wood Secondary School, London
Julia Coroama (12) 57
Emer Stevens (14) 58
Moresha Mariama Mansaray (13) 59
Ella Phillips (13) 60

Najibah Batanda (11) 60
Kate Alexandra Jevons (12) 61
James Hastings O'Shea (11) 62
Eliza Buckton (11) 62
Maya Muir (11) 63
Stan Webb (11) 63
Ellie Hutchings (12) 64
Yelena Jourdan-Wicker (11) 65
Amy Davis (13) 66
Tallulah Cox (12) 67
Maya Louise Kane (11) 68
Grace Heron (13) 68
Manon Elliott (11) 69
Laurie Logue (12) 70
Paddy Newcombe (11) 71
Dani Weiss (13) 71
Alex Matthew (13) 72
Yasmin Walton (13) 72
Louise Roberts (12) 73
Faber Bell (13) 73
Ruby Morgan (13) 74
Joshua Kingston (12) 75
Flo Stroud (11) 76
Erden Gungor (13) 76
Hakeem Edwards (11) 77
Tsiona Fernandes-Tadesse (12) 77
Layla Badalova (11) 78
Sophia Doncheff (14) 79
Victoria Stogdon-Culbert (13) 80
Olivia Dennis (12) 81
Shanya Braithwaite Ambrose (12) 82
Felix Andrew (11) 83
Ramneet Kaur Bains (13) 84
Yasemin Ozalcin (13) 85
Sophie Gill (12) 86
Mimi Brown (12) 86
Yousaf Khan (12) 87
Mia Blasi (13) 87
Tom Roberts (14) 88
Katya Dickson (11) 89
Zandile Mathebula-Jonah (13) 90
Jenasia Walker (11) 91
Selin Tas (13) 92
Amy Tafliku (13) 93
Evan Shute (11) 94
Rudi Wallis-O'Dowd (12) 94
Melissa Zara Kucuk (11) 95

Jessy Stoneman (12) 96
Amara C.J Blair (12) 97

Islamia Girls' School, London
Sumayah Halder (12) 97
Zainab Nawaz (11) 98
Maryam Zeeshan (12) 99
Zaynah Rashid (12) 99
Mahek Nadeem (11) 100
Dilara Duran (11) 101
Manaahil Ahmad (11) 102
Sarah Khawaja (11) 103
Parisay Mirza Safdar (12) 104
Aisha Fazil (12) 105
Hiba Ajwat Ul-Hasan (12) 106
Malaika Kashif (12) 107
Husna Hussain (12) 108
Hanin Hasib (11) 109
Manal Elgiathi (12) 109

Portland Place School, London
Loiena Emmett (14) 110
Lia Mordezki (13) 111
Oona Wolseley (13) 112
Louis Chalupa (14) 113
Katy Khoroshkovska (14) 114

Queensmead School, London
Ichhhca Rai (12) 114
Grace Wells (14) 115
Grace Emily Ridgeway (12) 116
Syed Hamza Hasan (13) 117
Narmin Safi (12) 117
Abigail Bunker (12) 118
Levi Yeo (12) 118
Rianna Christine Endersby (13) 119
Parkavi Gnanasundaram (13) 119
Ryan Silver (12) 120
Meghana Trivedi (12) 121
Sahil Patel 122
Lukas Serapinas (12) 123
Nurany Sawda Khan (12) 124
Zaheera Ghani (13) 125
Jack Penny (12) 125
Nataliya Klymko 126

Talmud Torah Tiferes Shlomoh, London
Yanky Deblinger (13) 126
Shimmy Grunfeld (13)................................127
Mordche Grosz (13) 127
Mendy Hus (13)...128

The Ellen Wilkinson School For Girls, London
Morsal Safi Sarajzada (17)..........................128

The John Roan School, London
Amy Pham (13) 129
Rael Lutaj (11)..129
Cindy Nguyen (13) 130
Nathan Biddlecombe-Nicolle (15) 130
Debor Adams (12) 131
Kai Sen (12) 131
Titiana Varca (11) 132
James Keating (12).....................................133
Chloe Tu (13) 134
Sulayman Ahmad-MacKinnon (13) 134
Tallulah Millman (12)..................................135
Charlie Sharpe (11).....................................136
Thomas Pratten (12)...................................136
Paradise Farr (11).......................................137
Morgen McCameron (11) 138
Ellie O'Mara (12) 139
Amy Pogson Jones (12) 140
Lucy-Anne Mitchell (12) 141
William Bullen (11).....................................141
Adam Tolfree (11).......................................142
Dylan Haynes (12)......................................142
Amelie Anne Denomme Watson (14).........143
Kiyan Mehre (12)..143
Erta Kupa (11)..144
Amber-Jade Hastings (11) 145
Muna Ahmedey (12)...................................146
Jai Cheung (11)..147
Eldona Kupa (13) 148
Esther Miller (14)..149
Shannon Dean (11) 149
Louise Collins (13)......................................150
Brenda Menyhart (13).................................151
Sayaka Bhandari (14).................................152
Erin Jade Morgan (13)................................153

Esther Joel (12)...154
George Stepan (12)....................................155
Rebecca Leigh (12).....................................156
Ella Maria Josefiina Leppänen (13)............157
Agata Morgan (12).....................................158
Joe Tuffee (11)...159
Olivia Melvin...159
Alfred Pryke (11)..160
Jamie Majomi (11)......................................161
Sophie May Prizeman (11).........................161
Amber Louise Pledge (11) 162

The Sacred Heart Language College, Harrow
Amy Carolan (12)..163
Sekura Queensborough (13).......................163
Carolina Isabel Vieira Fernandes (12).......164
Alicja Majewska (12)...................................165
Maggie Reddington (12)..............................165
Vanessa Litha Banda (12)...........................166
Jessica Maquiece Faty Mbala (12)..............167
Lauren John-Charles (13)...........................167
Lois O'Flaherty (12)....................................168
Nicole Moyo (13)...169
Essence Walters-Williams (12)...................170
Patrycja Lukasiewicz (14)...........................171
Isabella Dalpat (11)....................................172
Danielle Arday (12).....................................172
Nikola Anna Maciejowska (13)...................173
Kendi Hunter-Lander (11) 173
Rebecca Painter (11)..................................174
Holly Kellett Quince (11)............................175
Natalie Emmens (13)..................................176
Grace Hovey (12)..177
Mayá Wilson (11) 178
Mela Sarah Musie (11)...............................179
Eliana Padalino (13)...................................180
Grace Aleksandra McHugh (12) 181
Rachel Irabor (12).......................................182
Eleanor Horne (13).....................................183
Lorianne Swift (12).....................................184
Olivia Cole Keller (11) 185
Kanisha Kumaran (12)................................186
Cara McNally (11).......................................187
Elizabeth Adeyemi (12)...............................188

Tatianna-Rose Marie
Weymouth-Shanks (12) 188
Jenith Andrea Soundararajan (12)............189
Kaira George (13) 189
Georgine Albaque (13) 190
Jessica Odukwu (13) 191
Nadia Ampofo (13)..192
Jasmine Wadhwani (12).................................192
Eilis Bourke (12) 193
Shanai Ranasinghe (12)..................................193
Zoe Grace McCormack (12) 194
Milly Cooney (13) 195
Lauren Austin-Glass (11)................................196
Kayla Ivana Quarshie (12).............................196
Kacey June McDonald (11)...........................197
Jessica McIntyre (12).......................................197
Cassie Olympia Fernandes (11)...................198
Erin Pitts (12) 199
Olivia Inniss (12) 200
Frances Parkinson (11)...................................201
T'yana Nee-Chambers (12) 202
Isabel Earls..202
Thasini Doluweera Watta Gamage (11)..203
Amanda Tarka (11)..204
Klaudia Karolina Zajac (11) 205
Brianne Jade Conlon (11)..............................206
Izabela Dan (11)...207
Erica Sagoe (11)..208
Kerys Sian Manuel 209
Kimberley Osayande (11) 210
Elizabeth Moran (12) 211

THE POEMS

JEKYLL THE FOOL

I knew a boy named Hyde
He was a crazy fool,
He brought life and soul to the whole school
But at 2 o'clock every day, without a doubt
He was nowhere to be seen, not about.

Rumours say he turned into someone unrecognisable
Someone smart, clever, responsible
No more green hair, no more fool
Instead a plain dude named Jekyll.

In the night
Hyde returned
His hair showing the flames
His eyes burned
He was crazier every time
And the first sentence he spoke on solo line
'The night is mine.'
He flashed a smile and a dance, he said,
'There's two side to everyone and you're the same
It's just that mine likes to come out and play.'

Kaosi Mbaeri (14)

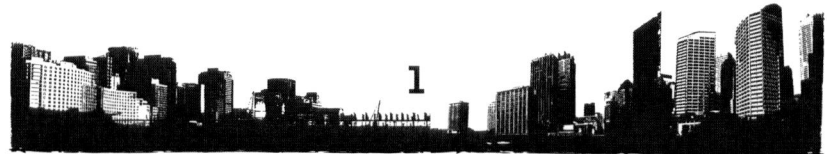

MY LIFE

See my friends dying, it's got me frightened,
crying, thinking, if it's a life that I'm finding

Got my grandma praying, she's stressing, still ain't learned my lesson,
surprised at birthday, even if I get one present, but she loves me,
been taking me to church from a little baby.

Never picked nor will I ever smoke weed, not trying to go to jail,
trying to live free

Got prayed for so many times, got to the point where I can't even deny,
Mum's stressing, can't sleep at night

If I gave a key to my heart, you can see the empty parts right back to the past,
thinking how long it will last,
I was brought up by my aunty, cousies and granny, not by my mummy,
I never see it sunny, always see dark, get angry very fast,
got people thinking that I'm nuts, but I messed up my life, but my grandma said,
'Pray and you will survive.'

Trying to live the best of me in the system, Mummy never took care of me,
sending two little messages on Facebook, said seen, never replied.

Tick-tock, when you going to come? When you going to explain?
When you going to make all this pain go away?
Got told back then that you were my mum, got told back then when I was having fun, then everything stopped, went downhill, no one ever asked how I felt.

I felt lonely, I felt sad, couldn't even turn to my dad, didn't want to know me,
left me in the hospital with my aunty, living in this nightmare, it's a fright, yeah,
can't even shed a tear, cos it's my life here, always doing bad from good,
when I know I shouldn't be, never want to hear the teacher clearly,

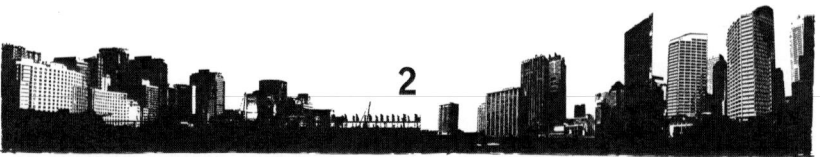

always want to be the clown in the class, having feelings trapped in my heart from the past,
but that ain't me, I'm a nice girl when I want to be, get to know me, get to join the family.
This is my life.

Paige Ricketts (14)
Abbey Manor College, London

THEY SEE, I SEE

They see a dark cloud passing by
And I see a weird gleam in their eyes
And I'm just thinking
Whilst I'm passing by

What's wrong with me
That you can't even smile?
You can't judge what you see
Until you get to know the real me

People think I'm loud
But I'm really just outspoken
And trying to get my words out

I'm just a girl in a big crowd
Trying to find her way out
I'm trying to be a better person
But it's not as easy as it seems
Because I keep hiding under these
coloured sheets

I wish people could just see me
for who I really am
Under the last remaining sheet over me
Beyond my 50 shades of black
is loyalty
Independence
and determination
and that's who I see when I look at me.

Miekella Grant-Irish (13)
Abbey Manor College, London

DAYS OF SPRING

The sun peeks out of the abominable cloud,
Its rays hitting the cold, frozen ground,
The abandoned soil is nurtured and cared
And the tree trunks are no longer bare.

A bird sings, a call, an alarm,
For nocturnal animals to come,
The scent of birth is in the air
And their homes are cordial and fair.

Plants tangle and fight against each other,
For the sun's faint kiss of summer,
The breeze catches a child's voice as she plays,
Awakening flowers; blossoming in the month of May.

Aiysha McInnes (13)
Acton High School, London

WHO AM I?

I have a ponytail every day,
I go to eat mostly hay,
I can usually smell people's emotions,
That is my magic potion,
I sometimes go in races,
And see many happy faces,
I can be in colours,
And please many mothers,
That is the end of me,
So try to guess who you'll see!

Rawan Badreddine (12)
Acton High School, London

THE MYSTERY OF THE OCEAN

The ocean is a lock,
We need to find the key,
There are so many parts of it we have never seen,
From colours to creatures that lurk in the night,
To dolphins and sharks that give you a fright.

The ocean goes deep,
Deeper than we know,
Even if you want to
You can't go too low.

People have fears of what they don't know,
Some people love it,
The ocean's quite a show.

If you look down into the darkness,
The mystery of the sea,
You might find yourself somewhere
You wish you had never been.

Ella Torbett (12)
Acton High School, London

GOLDEN TREASURE

'The treasure is mine,'
that's all I can say.
I need to find the treasure
by the end of the day,
Otherwise I'll be sad
in every way,
The only thing I need to do now
is pray!

Kweku Isaiah James Anoom (12)
Acton High School, London

A DAY IN THE PARK

As I tilt my head back, I see blue
Blue is a tragic story
A soggy day, damp yet dry
A child sobbing under the dark sky
An all alone puppy failing to impress
Life is sad, life is wretched

I see kids playing around
Their eyes bright and wet from laughter
Though mine are wet they are not from laughter
They are wet from sadness

The kids are now sitting on a bench
Poor kids
I remember when we used to come here
When we sat on benches, it usually meant that we
Were discussing something important
Such as the time you said that you wanted to be 'free'
I did not know what that meant then
That was the start of the ending

I wish I was there when it all happened
I wish I was there to save you.

Najma Abdulkadir (13)
Acton High School, London

THIS IS WHAT I DREAM TO BE

Waking up slowly,
going with what I see,
This is what I wish to be.

Going on adventures,
feeling free!
This is what I dream to be.

Watching sunsets.
laughing with glee,
This is what I dream to be.

Climbing the Alps,
speeding with skis,
This is what I wish to be.

Exploring the ocean,
sailing the sea,
This is what I wish to be.

Filling my days,
being happy,
This is what I wish to be.

That's not all,
only a few,
There is more that I wish to be.

Evan Spencer (13)
Acton High School, London

FRACTURED FACE

A fractured face,
A broken soul,
Eyes cracked,
Mouth snapped,
Nothing is whole,
Nothing is right,
Never to be fixed,
This face is broken,
The mirror reflects this,
Broken but still round,
Shards of glass,
Flaking away,
Into oblivion; darkness.
The light never to be cast
On this ever broken,
Fractured face.

Francesca Birri (13)
Acton High School, London

A MESSAGE TO GERMANY

When photographs were published of Londoners,
They were never looking gloomy or depressed,
Never looking fed up or exhausted,
Or wearied by the lack of rest.

The mood was always one of optimism,
Bombed out we may be, but we're not down,
We'll do anything to keep our spirits up,
Show everyone a smile and not a frown.

We can take it, so Germany do your worst,
You're mistaken if you think you can win,
All that you can do will never be enough,
The British people will never give in.

Baraa Sheryanna (12)
Acton High School, London

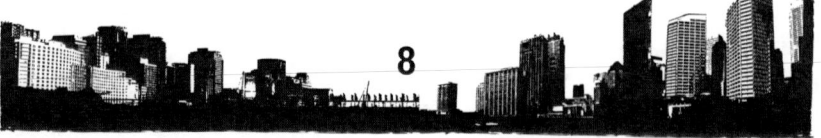

WHY

Just stop and think why,
why is one word everyone has used,
why do we say bye?
To acknowledge someone's leaving I guess.

When someone says why, the answers are infinite,
but sometimes no one knows the answer
and we're just left to guess,
sometimes out guesses are close, but normally they're miles away.

Why can be annoying through,
when you know and answer but want to keep it a secret,
people will pester you for it, repeating the word why,
till you give up and tell them.

Why is a mystery,
it is the unknown,
waiting to be found,
just think, you could be the one to find it.

Caitlin May Wales (13)
Acton High School, London

FATHER AT WAR

Every day I wait for him, it fills me with stress,
If you don't think so, then imagine your father on the battlefield.
Imagine if he died, you would be scared.
I digress.
The sounds of gunfire are haunting me every day,
Ever since my father went to war for D-Day.
Now all I can do is play with my garden gnomes,
Until the day my father finally comes home.

Leon Gjata (13)
Acton High School, London

BOOKS

Run your fingers across the shelf of paperbacks,
Carefully extract the words,
Encased in a glossy, blue jacket.

Open it and let the world immerse you,
Images of forests and magic are conjuring up in your mind,
Feel pity for the character who doesn't have a clue.

Inhale the smell of musty paper,
Forget all reality,
Everything that is true.

Long to jump in amongst it all,
To be able to wave a wand and create sparks,
Wish for a fire-breathing dragon.

Close it up,
Put it away
And return for the rest of the day.

Aggie Bright (13)
Acton High School, London

SURVIVAL OF THE FITTEST

Snakes are coated in camouflage,
While the rhinos lower their horns to charge,
It's the survival of the fittest,
You need to be the biggest,
Survival of the fittest!

Tigers snarl and bare their teeth,
Skunks can ward off evil with their reeking stench,
It's the survival of the fittest,
You need to be the nastiest,
Survival of the fittest!

Eagles snatch prey up with their razor claws,
Jaguars prancing on their unheard paws,
It's the survival of the fittest,
You need to be the meanest,
Survival of the fittest!

Andre Arnaoudov (11)
Acton High School, London

THE POWER OF FRIENDSHIP

How could a man survive without friendship,
If one was to trip up on Mount Everest, who would save him?
A trusty, loyal friend.

How could a child survive without friendship,
If one was bullied in school who would save him?
A comforting, helpful friend.

How could a man survive without friendship,
If one was to follow his dream and fail who would be there to save him?
A supportive, encouraging friend.

How could a man survive without friendship,
If one was on the brink of self-destruction who would save him?
A caring, worried friend.

How could a man survive without friendship,
If one was to lose all hope in something who would save him?
A persevering, optimistic friend.

There's only one way a human being could survive without normal friendship,
If one was to have all the problems above, so you know who would be there?
A best friend.

Jaydon Goodfellow (12)
Acton High School, London

THE DEEP BLUE

As I walked along the path,
Every sound giving me a fright,
The moon a face of ghoulish delight,
The only sign of welcoming light.

The sea splashed violently on the rocks,
The white froth angrily reaching out to the seagull flocks,
As I got down, looking at the sea,
I crouched down on one knee,
As I got swept away.

The wind whistled,
The boat groaned,
The sky dismissed it and became day.

Since then I've been taken wherever the 'Deep Blue' wanted me to go,
North, south, east, west, fast or slow,
I never tired of the oceans,
There was never a big commotion,
Relaxing, I thought.

A big wave hits me, knocking me down,
I go deeper, deeper, the sun glistening on the blue surface,
I'm out of breath, so I sleep deep.
The slumber encases me.
I never wake up.

Emily Laura Page (11)
Acton High School, London

THE HORRORS OF WAR

Side by side, we walk towards our fate,
You can hear the gas shells
dropping softly behind.

All of us scrambling for our oversized masks,
I saw him drowning slowly in misty fog,
collapsing onto the rock hard ground.

We marched on, leaving a soldier behind.

We reached a sea of blood and limbs,
so horrifying worlds could not describe.
Many had already lost their lives.

Bang! He died, nothing can compare to
seeing your comrade fall to their death.
A wound that has scarred me for life.

For anyone desperate for glory,
this is not the way!

Ifrah Hussain (12)
Acton High School, London

PASSING ANTHEM

As I lie here on the edge,
Through my ears run terrified screams,
Through my veins runs my desperate pledge.

Around me explodes the blood and bones
Of those who were once my friends,
But all I see is a blinding light,
As I lay and accept my end.

The cries don't seem too wretched now,
The pain is starting to lull,
My friends don't seem too desperate now,
It doesn't hurt, I don't know how.

And for some strange reason,
I feel a sense of relief,
When I open my eyes and see the poppies,
I'm buried knees deep in.

As I trudge through my wonderland,
All I hear is my anthem
And from the corner of my eye, I spy my old friends,
As I limp in sorrow to greet them.

Ella Edwards (12)
Acton High School, London

TOO MUCH TECH

No matter how much tech we have,
There is no such thing as enough.
Even if we make a robot,
They insist on making it tough.
Flying cars, a trip to Mars,
A walking, talking bass guitar.
Maybe a jetpack with loads of guns,
or duplicate our own sun.
A computer as big as the Eiffel Tower,
Or a phone with unlimited power.
Scientists believe in the dream of tech,
Maybe a watch on your neck.
Buy a house in space,
Or find a new planet, a new place.
But what if tech isn't good?
Could it turn everything into sand,
And make Earth a wasteland?
Could it be useful or could it be the end?
Is tech really just a false friend?
The real question is, is there too much tech?
There's only one way to find out!

Hassan Edaan (12)
Acton High School, London

THE ABNORMAL CHILD

Within me I believe,
The dark overwhelms my light,
Bursting to awaken,
Waiting for my brain's vulnerable moment,
At this point the mind is no longer sane,
Fear and hatred dominate my membrane,
Gothic emotions engulf me,
In a never-ending attempt to be accepted,
To be trusted and loved,
But that can never happen.
Mental isn't quite the word to describe it,
Deranged, perplexed is what people call me,
In school I see only darkness,
Joy is an empty feeling,
Which is replaced with despair,
I seem and act differently,
Even though it's not my fault,
I get blamed for my 'anti-social behaviour',
Well that's what my psychologist told me,
I feel like my opinion doesn't matter,
There's only one way to describe myself;
Abnormal...

Jamal Mohamed (13)
Acton High School, London

A MOTHER'S GLUE

You are my life support
I wouldn't survive without you
You tell me to hold my head high
But the pain is too real
You told me what you went through
I told you too
You told me to hold my head high
What will I do?
You told me about my first steps
You told me about my tumbles
I told you about my heartbreaks
You gave me some glue
The glue eventually dried
My heart mended
All because of you.

Lamiah Persaud-Hibbert (12)
Acton High School, London

THE FIRST DAY OF ACTON HIGH SCHOOL

The first day at Acton High
I was scared and nervous
I wanted to go back home
I didn't know anyone
Just my old friends from primary school
But none of them were with me in class.
I met new students but I didn't know them
This is what happened on my first day at Acton High School.

Somaya Damhoun (11)
Acton High School, London

THE FUTURE

The future is a wonderful time
always a shining star in the sky.

The brilliant technology really
surprises me.
4D phones and hoverboards,
illuminate the world around me.

The land will be floating
alongside the moon, humans and animals will inhabit this paradise,
the brand new iPhone 25
which will be able to transport you
to another planet outside Earth.

I just can't wait for the new technology,
people will have mansions hovering
in such a different place
with an electronic remote which
makes you travel anywhere.

There's going to be such blinding stuff
that you won't even notice when days are changing.

Money will be used more often
and you will be so amazed
when there's communicating robots everywhere.

I just can't wait for the amazing future.

Dawud Mazidi (12)
Acton High School, London

MY CRYSTAL-CLEAR MOTHER

You are my everything,
I don't know what I would do without you,
you help me with my problems
and you do everything for me.

You feed me,
care for me,
I tell you about my problems,
you hug me with your warm hands,
I don't know what I would do without you.

My mother is my angel,
she works hard to care for me,
my mother is my guardian for life,
I don't know what I would do without her.

I love my mother.

Zuzanna Rakowska (12)
Acton High School, London

WAR POEM

The sound of the fallen cry
each gunshot sounding deafening
for some it is honourable to die
as this is the day of reckoning.

Step by step, the soldiers go
one single movement is threatening
whatever weather, even snow
for this is the day of reckoning.

Is it all worth it in the end?
All this fighting, it's just sickening
nothing but more funerals to attend
as this is the day of reckoning.

Though in the end some shall survive
some young minds just developing
fallen, wishing to be alive
as the bodies on the day of reckoning.

Akram Kassim (13)
Acton High School, London

MUSIC

Music, calming music, soothes you, loses you,
It can anger you, it can make you happy.
Music is a lot of things
but really we all love it.
Pop, rap, country...
all these different types
but don't we all wonder what it all means?

Music helps us, confuses us.
Inspirational, unhelpful?
All these questions we want to ask -
but we can't.
Music is what you make it,
so make sure you listen to the words...

M ajestic,
U nhelpful,
S oothing,
I nspirational,
C alming.

Shaniyah Blake Eccleston (11)
Acton High School, London

INANIMATY

Inanimate objects are forks,
Inanimate objects are corks,
Inanimate objects there are a lot, they can also even be sporks.

But what if they don't exist?
Inanimaty, I'm talking about this,
If everything had feelings, even this drawing of a fish.

Everything might have feelings,
The book you were just in the library reading,
The chair you're sitting on now, the banana you might have been peeling.

Now I don't see how,
How it exists now,
Maybe, in the future, maybe in the past, but now I don't see how.

Inanimaty is a noun,
A word it must be bound,
Inanimate is an adjective and I know what it's not,
Inanimate isn't a noun.

Inanimaty isn't a word,
This whole poem is absurd,
Inanimate is a word that exists,
So this piece of paper won't care if the last line doesn't rhyme,
And has too many syllables.

Joshua Carr (11)
Acton High School, London

THE BEAUTIFUL GAME

Every boy's dream is to play football,
Nightly kicking the ball against the wall
And when Saturday comes around,
A few new players will be found.
Whether it's Arsenal or Fleetwood Town,
When the game's lost you will frown.

If the big break comes,
Then you won't be in school doing sums,
Money will be pouring in,
While others are eating out of a bin
And if you get an injury,
Some will have sympathy.

When you've been at the physio,
It'll be surprising if you even make a cameo
And then, that'll be your career,
Life was well spent!

Alfred Davis (12)
Acton High School, London

MINECRAFT ACROSTIC

M is for mining, you'll do this a lot
I is for iron, from ore to ingot
N is for Nether, a whole new world
E is for Ender dragon with its tail in a curl
C is for coal, a good source of fuel
R is for rabbits, kill them you are cruel
A is for anvil, used to repair
F is for fish, hardly ever there
T is for tomorrow and a brand new day,
   on Minecraft to create, fight and play.

Matthew Smart (11)
Acton High School, London

HEART CHASER, HEART SEEKER, HEART PURSUER

Another day gone
A degree of apathy
Though only to an extent

Flooded on the stairs
Drowning on drops and drizzles
You were all alone

Tried to comfort you
Despite your other ideas
Another bullet

Pierces through my soul
The battles always choose me
Yet never destroyed

What is your name son?
Your guess is as good as mine
My heart's uphill war

Cold blood seeps from me
It scampers on the river
Scurry to rescue

Wrestle the rapids
No tide will ever down me
Survive the upsurge

Scream to the currents
Rocks the tide and rides the waves
Time to levitate

Smash through the fourth wall
Out bursts a shimmering light
With warmth from the heart

Summon your power
Pump your heart's veins with fire
Fight with desire.

Kasem Oakley (16)
Acton High School, London

THE STARVING WOLF

He prowled around the luscious greenery,
His mind solely focused on food,
The cunning assassin's ears perked up,
Leaves crashed in the background,
He ran as fast as a bullet,
Pursuing his one and only chance,
Hunger and tiredness soon overwhelmed the wolf,
The rare meal vanished,
As she slowly panted and turned away.

His weakness was hunger,
His enemy was tiredness,
Gently, the weary wolf stumbled away,
Impossible!
The hunter spotted a juicy, plump rabbit in front of him,
He was aware that this would end his never-ending battle against hunger.
The chase began,
He was determined to capture this rabbit,
Hunger was not going to disturb him now.
For a while he growled and moaned,
He stared into the prey's weak eyes,
His stomach persuaded him to carry on,
Begging his muscles to not give up.

At last, the body was rewarded
And hunger and tiredness abolished.

Mohamed Ali (13)
Acton High School, London

I'M IRISH

I'm Irish, I'm Irish,
I do Irish dance,
if you listen I'll give you a chance.

I live in Dublin, it's where I'm from,
I've tried Kimberly's, Tatos and a lot more.

I'm Irish, I'm Irish,
I am, I am very Irish living in Ireland.

My family is Irish
and so am I, they come from
Limerick, Kerry and Cork.

I'm Irish, Irish,
if you find a four-leaved clover
you're in for good luck, the luck of the Irish.

In Ireland, in Ireland,
there are loads of famous rivers,
like the River Shannon.

I'm Irish, I'm Irish,
proud to say,
I will always be Irish every day!

Kayla Hughes (11)
Acton High School, London

CHICKEN

C overed in crispy skin
H elpless to resist
I mpossible to replace
C arefully taking tiny bites to enjoy the most of it
K nowledge providing taste
E ndless enjoyment
N ever-ending thirst for chicken

A t the top forever
N othing beats chicken
D ying for more

C hasing after chips
H ungrier with every chip I put in my mouth
I nterior shiny and delicate
P osh flavour with a touch of ketchup sauce
S ergio loves his chicken and chips.

Sergio Srowronski (12)
Acton High School, London

UNTITLED

I love you and you love me
We could be a family
I can see me in your eyes
There's no way I could disguise
All these crazy thoughts in my mind now.
I turn you on, I play COD on you,
I like games, you like them too,
This is why we should be together
Because without you, I am a feather.
When I ask you this question
Please say yes,
'Will you marry me you beautiful princess?'
I love you and you love me,
We should be a family.
I love you.

Nilkanth Kalan (11)
Acton High School, London

THE SPELL

Double, double, toil and trouble,
Fire burn and cauldron bubble.

Ice to water, change and turn,
Fishes' gills and thou shalt learn.

Rotten teeth and raven's claws,
Ostrich slime and puppies' paws.

Darkness seeps where once was fun,
Dolls under bed, the deed is done.

Ground to sky and sky to ground,
What you seek shall not be found.

With the mind of a mage and a warrior's rage,
You'll be at last freed from your cage.

Taiyyabah Khan (13)
Deptford Green School, London

CRYING MEMORIES

Come home, it's 4 o'clock,
See my mom sitting and crying.
So I asked, 'Are you OK?
Why are you crying?'
She said it was my uncle; he was dead.
I said, 'How? Why? He was so young.'
She said, sobbing, I couldn't really make it out,
I think she said, 'It was heroin.'
I couldn't believe it.
I never knew death was something you could not escape,
You cannot prevent it,
But you can deal with it.

Anastacia Mary Koncz (15)
Deptford Green School, London

THE HISTORICAL CITY

I still remember the streets
I can still smell the river
The waves sound against the coast
The important history about my city.
The city where I was born
The sea eagles flying on top like a storm;
This is my city.

The country it is in
The beautiful country is the place where I was born.
My dear people are still there
They are far away from me
But I can still feel their love for me.

Michele Cascella (15)
Deptford Green School, London

OUR WORLD

We live in a world
Where everything
We do is determined
By our environment.

No matter what
Lifestyle we choose.
No matter what
We want to be,
It is still determined by
What we see
Other people do.

Even when we
Think we are
Being original and
We are doing
What we want,
We actually aren't.

We are so blinded
By our society;
When will we
Get to be what we
Want to be?
When will we get to live
How we want to live
And not get criticised?

Princess Dumenu (15)
Deptford Green School, London

MY PAST TO THE FUTURE

When I was young I wanted to be
A fashion designer.
I came home from nursery, bringing paintings, drawings and creative things,
to my smiling mum.
She was so happy every time she came to collect me,
So I grew up thinking that I would be
A fashion designer,
Drawing and colouring the pictures I drew.

Now, I am here thinking of
The past and the future,
Changed my mind, now I want to be
A hairdresser,
To run a business of my own.
Thinking of the future scares me,
In case of failing or getting stuck
And your dream not being achieved.

And when the future comes
I will be a well-qualified woman,
Running my business,
Building a new family and new lives.
I will achieve my dream and die,
With happiness in my life.

Adelina Ajrizaj (15)
Deptford Green School, London

THE DREAM I DREAM

Just like Martin Luther King, I too have a dream,
My dream is different, but still as powerful as a raging bull.
My dream can move a thousand soldiers,
That's the dream I dream.

The dream I dream moves swiftly as
A light feather, but my dream can be
Dark and aggressive.
My dream tells a story.
'History is a river that flows to the sea,
Laced with the bone of memory'
That's the dream I dream.

The dream I dream is a living nightmare,
But without the monsters under your bed, or
The shadow that looks like a huge, dark figure,
But is only a tree.
Nightmares are just my evil side,
That I can't control,
But now I realise
I am the dream that I dream.

Kareem Harris (15)
Deptford Green School, London

I DREAM...

I dream...
Of a world where peace is sovereign
where life strikes at wars and famines
and every Earth born child
will greet the world with adoration

I dream...
That the news will provide us with
uplifting, inspiring stories
instead of murder cases
and people don't debate
whether we should let more refugees into the country

I dream...
That people don't judge other people by...
the way they dress
their skin colour
or the texture of their hair

I dream...
that people do not judge other people by...
their stereotypes
our faith
their genders
our way to look
the stereotypes that people fabricate!

I dream...

Denise Victoria Lawrence (11)
Deptford Green School, London

WILD

My emotions in the future, I drown
In my tears, thinking about my
Sorrows, crying about my fears.
On my happy days, I love
The fast lane and my emotions
Go wild into fifth gear.

Every day I shed a tear, I realise
What a great future I have ahead
And smile, then look deep into
My emotions and think about
My future being pitied.

These emotions going wild
Like an untamed cat,
Acting like a child...
My future going wild.

And so I think I'm mild
Reminiscing about my childhood.
I think about my peers and fly up
In the sky, just to realise it's all
Clear.

What I want to be in the future,
I know and I have seen it
Before, but I conclude and
Say my emotions are poor and
Wild like a baby child.

Josh Heloussala (15)
Deptford Green School, London

THE NIGHTMARE

Start on my back, eyes closed,
Hoping for, expecting even
A good dream.
A dream of peace and one from which
I wake refreshed.

But this one is a nightmare,
I fall headlong into it,
I feel small,
I don't know if I am small
Or everything else is huge.
Things run after me;
The closer I get to escape
The further away it seems.

Dreams can be problematic to express,
Some things there are no words for.
Indescribable.

I dream every night, or so they say,
But these are the ones I remember.

Bailey Peden (15)
Deptford Green School, London

SECONDS

I fell off my bike
(One moment I was on and then not)
For three whole seconds, my elbow furiously scraped the ground.
I softly touched my arm as tears rolled down my face.

My friends were nearby,
They took me home.
My mum tucked me into bed and said,
'We'll see if it gets better - hospital in the morning.'
Hospital. Uncertainty. Fear.

I was five and a half.

Kieran Appleby (14)
Deptford Green School, London

SPACE

Space,
it's weird what nothing can do to you,
gasping for air before you become frozen through
and just in absence of air and ground
you are drifting, dead, no way to be found
but we don't tend to think of space as a genocidal maniac
but more of a space with things it does rather lack
for a life to go on as a human being
but when you're floating in space, take a look at the nothingness you're seeing.

Space,
though the dark and cold vacuum of space seems rather dull and dark
try to remember that light is all around you from a nearby star
coming flying through the cold and into your heart
but light is a very funny thing travelling so fast
it took us thousands of years to realise it actually travelled past
but if you're in the nothing of space the light won't help you from your fate.

Space
now I know this poem seems rather depressing
but this is the main point I'll be addressing
and that cold vacuum of nothing is nothing
that can't be conquered by mind and heart and this is not bluffing
even if we keep our feet Earthbound
Our changes can make differences on interstellar ground
and you is just the beginning
with time on our side, we will be winning, even if we are just a small part of space
and this is not restricted by gender or race.

James Casey (12)
Forest Hill School, London

NEVER LOSE FAITH

In life, there is never a time when God leaves our side,
all you got to do is trust in Him and the bad times will disappear.
Never lose hope in God,
He blessed everyone with a magical elf.
The little friend will help you in times of distress,
he will lead you where you ought to go,
cos he knows best
And when you find yourself completely lost, without a clue,
just smile and then a new door will open for you.

Nana Boahene (12)
Forest Hill School, London

JIM

There once was a man called Jim,
He liked to live in a bin,
He had no kin,
But had his gin,
And a tatty old violin.

His playing was terribly bad,
It made the public sad,
They cried, 'Oh dear Jim!
Are you making that din?
Should have stayed in the bin!'

Jack Morrish (13)
Forest Hill School, London

THE CAGED BIRD

For the caged bird sings of freedom
He is captured for no good reason
He still sings from the lungs out loud
As he is a part of a caged bird crowd
The uncaged use them as tools
They have no knowledge, they didn't go to school
They are mistreated like they aren't even birds
Your life will be ended without a word.

We aren't given beneficial food, instead we are given just wheat
The only thing keeping us going is our little heartbeat
We are overlooked by the rich swan
He treats them like a game, but this isn't fun
But every day the caged bird sings for freedom
All together, in unison
One big family, all behind bars
Where the other families live ever so far
They are bought and sold like discarded toys
And taken to a family with mums, dads and young little boys
They are beaten, whipped, smacked into shape
But the caged bird sings for freedom once again.

Travis Burchell (14)
Forest Hill School, London

THE CRAZY WAY HOME!

Now open your eyes and gaze into the futuristic pictures,
You are surrounded by all kinds of adventures.
Look around yourself, around your handsome features,
The paths you go along are lined with shining natures,
Around the world, discovering different creatures.

Now walking into the school seeing students having sessions,
Waiting for teachers to finish registration.
Sometimes teachers can forget their presentations
And this makes students have poor reputations,
Even the art teachers, wondering what's creation?

Now coming to a roundabout, where traffic lights are red, yellow, green,
Two racing motorbikes seeing who gets to win.
Crazy Porsche and Lamborghini crashing into a bin
And the children, from schools nearby,
Go on the crosswalk when the school bells ring,
And the bell ringing, dllliiiiing!

Now tiptoeing into the magnificent beach,
The shiny, bright sea, salted and rich.
A soft blow dragged the wave onto the land as far as no more than an inch,
People sitting on a deckchair, below a sunshade eating peach,
With a market selling them, fifty pence each.

Now creeping up the Mount Everest,
The view up there seems great and the best,
Lying on the tip of Everest having a rest,
Looking up on a bird struggling to find her nest
And then I made the choice of continuing my way home, the journey to the west.

Now arriving at my destination,
Looking for my generation,
Trying to bring back my reputation
And fill the whole world with cooperation.

Kewen Wang
Forest Hill School, London

THE DREAM...

As I slowly tiptoed on the floor,
creaks suspiciously came from the door!

Shivers instantly ran down my spine,
I convinced myself that everything was going to be fine!

I automatically felt like this was the end of my life,
It already felt like I was being stabbed with a knife.

Whispers softly rubbed against my ear
And that was a sign that danger was near!

Werewolves were
Howling,
Men were
Shouting,
My face was
Frowning.

I just had to accept that this wasn't fake,
I had to take risks I didn't want to
Take!

Suddenly,
I woke up in my bed and there were no memories left in my head!

Marc Morgan (11)
Forest Hill School, London

UNWANTED CHANGE

Life can be amusing,
Have you ever wished your teachers or coaches were better?
That they would be less harsh and less confusing
And be more supportive and be a better advisor?

Imagine if they left and you received a new one,
Wouldn't it be interesting?
No more assignments on brain-scrambling mathematic equations,
No more laps around the court.

But then you begin to see a change,
From within,
You start to lack what you once had,
The motivation to not be punished,
Without it,
There is no achievement
And you begin to fail with no way back to the top.

Sometimes we may want change,
But do we always need change?

Kang Mbang (12)
Harris City Academy Crystal Palace, London

FORM OF CHANGE

Everywhere you go you bring some form of change,
Everywhere the journey of life seems a little strange...

There are two main roles in your journey
You are the one who chooses which one to be
Either 'to be changed' or 'the change'
Both roles meet and rearrange

Where all good and bad people come your way
It doesn't mean that the good ones are there to stay;
The bad ones will pester and annoy you
They will stick to your mind like glue

When they are around
Don't let them hit the ground
They surround you all the time
So just smile and soon they will mime

Everywhere you go you bring some form of change,
Everywhere the journey of life seems a little strange!

Katerina Kennedy (12)
Harris City Academy Crystal Palace, London

CHANGE PLEASE

'Change please', I cried,
'Change please', I sighed.

Spare me some change
And I'll show you my musical range.
Change can add up to notes in money,
So I'll play you some notes as sweet as honey.

Give me a chance as a refugee,
Give me a chance I plea,
Like you, I once had a family too,
I had a home, a child, but all I have now is a damp shoe.

Money, money makes the world spin round,
So please have a heart of gold and lend me a pound.
Please, just once more let me sleep safe and sound,
Rather than leave me lying on the cold, hard ground.

'Change please,' I cry,
'Change please,' I sigh.

Anika Collins (11)
Harris City Academy Crystal Palace, London

CHANGE!

Get me a fan because it's hot in here
And the chilly breeze seems to have disappear
But when the burning season ends, it's always a bummer
Say farewell to the sun, say farewell to the summer

The days get colder, the trees grow older
And the leaves fall from trees up high
Trees bear bare bark
Soon it gets dark
I'll see you next autumn, bye!

Brr! It's cold, get me a sweater!
Precipitation falls down, wetter and wetter
The icy icicles form, sharp like a splinter
But soon, sadly, they melt and alas no more winter

Big, blooming bulbs
New life is created
It's lukewarm, not scorching
Summer is overrated
As the crops begin to grow,
For the nearing autumn harvest
Spring is lagging behind, once again, summer's passed us

The year restarts, let the cycle begin
Be patient for now, this year's story is *fin*!

Kirsti Jones (11)
Harris City Academy Crystal Palace, London

THAT IS CHANGE

She looks in the mirror,
And she sees a reflection as clear as crystal,
Reflection of a young girl, bold and beautiful,
From childhood to adulthood... change, that is modification.

Now she has started dressing cool,
Umm, is it because she's started high school?
Reflection of a young girl, bold and beautiful,
From childhood to adulthood... change, that is transition.

She walks down the streets alone, without holding her mum's hand,
Bold and proud, she is no child,
Reflection of a young girl, bold and beautiful,
From childhood to adulthood... change, that is innovation!

Jamiliah Oppong (11)
Harris City Academy Crystal Palace, London

CHANGE IN SEASONS

Winter is a time for blizzards and snow
And for baking lovely, fresh, home-made dough.
For putting on your warm, fluffy mittens
And cuddling up with your soft, purring kittens.

Spring is a time for blossoming flowers
And putting away all those cold winter hours.
From getting a kiss of the warm spring breeze
To the time of year where you meet all the busy bees.

Summer is the time for hot rays of sun
And for big and small kids to have tonnes of fun.
This is time where there's not a single muddy puddle,
But if you did see one, you would get in a muddle.

Autumn is a time for golden leaves,
And for all the big hibernating trees.
When summer draws its last warm breath
And autumn begins its long, cold trek.

Then, back around to winter
With blizzards and snow!

Ita Hermine Neumeyer (12)
Harris City Academy Crystal Palace, London

THE WORLD IS CHANGING

The winds came soaring
And the waters were raging,
the ground started to shake
Bringing waves to the lake,
The world was changing.

Bang! The houses started to break,
Bringing waves to the lake
And the world became opaque,
Darkness overpowered the light
As gloomy as the night,
The world was changing.

And then it hit us,
It was an earthquake,
The animals started to drop
As though time had come to a stop.
We all began to shiver
And the earth began to quiver,
The world was changing.

The oceans flooded the area,
Swarms of mosquitoes hit us,
We thought we would catch malaria,
All that was left was a tiny toy bus,
The world was changing.

The world was being devoured
By a beast, so overpowered,
Could we stop it?
We could not; and so the human race became a giant pit.
It was the end of the human race,
We had lost an endless chase,
The world had changed!

Riaz Pathan (12)
Harris City Academy Crystal Palace, London

CHANGES

Change affects me,
It affects you,
It affects everybody too.
Some people go,
Some people stay,
Some people go with the flow
And some get lost along the way.
Changes,
They go in steps,
They go in stages,
But everything changes.
Change affects me.

Jamilah Alisha Williams (12)
Harris City Academy Crystal Palace, London

CHANGES

Life is unpredictable,
It changes with the seasons,
Even the coldest winter
Happens for the best of reasons
And though it feels eternal,
Like all you'll ever do is freeze,
I promise spring is coming and with it brand new leaves.
Things are growing every moment,
All the night and day,
Things are changing all around us,
In a hundred different ways.
Can't you see the seasons changing?
Winter is turning into spring,
Can you hear the birds announce it?
Listen to them sing!

Zoe Donkor (12)
Harris City Academy Crystal Palace, London

A NEW BEGINNING

Starvation, we're on the brink,
We prayed to Allah we wouldn't sink,
For the sea was rough and the journey tough.

We stumbled off the boat, which fired up our hope,
For the land sweeter than Maamoui bi Ajwa.

We searched for asylum with no success,
This journey was turning into a terrible mess.

We walked through Greece, Serbia and Bosnia too,
Disease spreading, killing me and you.

Coughing and spluttering we made it to Calais,
Our decreasing budget causing dismay.

We hid in a lorry, not showing our worry,
This was it, do or die,
This was it, drop or fly.

We had made it to Dover,
Our journey over?

We now live in London, my mother and I
And why did we come here? I'll tell you why,

Because London is kind and London is free,
Because London is fair and London is me.

Theo Chapman (12)
Harris City Academy Crystal Palace, London

LIFE CHANGES

From egg to baby,
Chubby as a guinea pig,
I was extremely big!

From baby to toddler,
A lively bundle of joy,
Oh how I wouldn't share my beloved toy.

From toddler to child,
Calm, collected and cool,
I finally began my adventure at school.

From child to tween,
Zip went my faux fur bag,
I always wanted the latest mag.

From tween to teen,
I *begged* for luscious make-up,
I never wanted to wake up...

From teen to adult,
It was time to leave the nest
And I was a blubbery mess!

From adult to elderly,
I miss my old childhood,
If I could turn back time, I *really* would!

From me to you.

Rosanne Choong (12)
Harris City Academy Crystal Palace, London

THE CHANGE THAT WAR BRINGS

The guns are put down,
The militant's opinion swaying around,
Jerries surrendering,
The people are celebrating,
The war is over,
They didn't even see the White Cliffs of Dover!

Enemies become friends,
The end of the war is truly a godsend,
Europe's changing,
Into something completely new,
Austria, Hungary, goodbye to you!

Entente victorious,
Axis surrendered,
The German economy is failing,
Their money worth nothing,
Europe is turning to a new page,
Oh what a change!

Daniel May (13)
Harris City Academy Crystal Palace, London

CHANGE

Change can spark a moment,
Change can wake a dream,
Change can start a new life,
Change can be the same for you and me.

Change can build a friendship,
Change can enlighten a soul,
Change can guide a person,
Change can obtain a goal.

Change can change a nation,
Change can lift a room,
Change can wipe out darkness,
Change can conquer gloom.
Change can change two lives,
Change can make love bloom.

Change can start a journey,
Change can show you it's not rare,
Change can raise our spirits,
Change can show that you care,
But change can kill people,
So with that it brings despair.

Humzah Mohomed (13)
Harris City Academy Crystal Palace, London

ONLY IF

I woke up,
Small shimmers of sunlight slipped under my eyelids,
As I drew the curtains, my heart sank,
The tinged, rosy glow of the morning sun
Drenched me in joy,
For a while...

I listened,
For Dad dragging his suitcase solemnly off
The top shelf and bouncing down the stairs.
'Summer, time for eggs and beans,' called Dad
With a lump in his throat.
It was my favourite,
But not anymore...

I saw,
Mum walking into the bathroom with a white
band across her fourth finger,
She tried to hide her tears,
But her smudged mascara betrayed her,
I always cried with her,
To comfort her...

Only two words cross my mind,
Two words that if said at the time,
Could have changed everything;
Only if...

Jai Sood (13)
Harris City Academy Crystal Palace, London

THE YEAR HAS CHANGED

The cold, lifeless leaves begin to fall,
Off the trees that are so tall,
Bare branches and twigs are all that's left,
Nothing around... like the scene of a theft.
All children waiting for that moment where,
Incredibly, white snow fills the air,
It covers such a big range,
But so the weather will change!

The snow begins to fade
And all the snowmen that have been made,
Now fall to the ground,
Smiles turn to frowns,
Sun is upcoming,
Until they realise spring is coming!

Flowers begin to bloom,
People now turn off the heating in their rooms,
The warmth of the sun is a relief for most,
Summer is getting oh so close,
Smiles are on people's faces,
As they start to take more relaxed paces,
Now leaves begin to reappear,
Summer is here!

Shorts and T-shirt weather,
When neighbourhood barbecues bring people together,
Don't let the others get you down,
Because summer is the best part of all year round!

Ulrich Petri-Dawes (11)
Harris City Academy Crystal Palace, London

SEASONS

The kind of weather that clings to your skin,
The kind that makes all the birds sing,
The kind that might give you a tan,
The kind that makes you need a fan,
The kind that makes the bees all buzz,
The kind that has a soft, warm touch,
Summer has gone, autumn has arrived now, it's a different season's time.

The clouds comfort the sky,
Not many birds fly by,
The leaves begin to fall,
The colours of red, orange, green and more,
Animals go on a hunt,
To find their monthly lunch,
Autumn has gone, winter has arrived now, it's a different season's time.

Everyone is sound a sleep,
Snow is four feet deep,
You wake up to a row of frosted cakes,
Only to see the cars covered by snowflakes,
You drink a cup of warm soup,
Even if it tastes like gloop.
Winter has gone, spring has arrived now, it's a different season's time.

The snow melts away,
The flowers begin to blossom,
The trees stretch out their arms to welcome the sun,
Hoping that no more rain will come,
The stars come out at night to say goodbye to all four season's times.

Zaina-Rene Hannah Francis (11)
Harris City Academy Crystal Palace, London

THE WOODS

I walked into the woods,
I stared at it gradually,
as it stared back.
The rain pattered,
the rain drizzled.
The rain, the worst thing
I don't even know
what I did wrong.
I had no power,
I had no strength,
all that was left of me
was a long silence.
Again,
it watched me,
I watched it back.
It ended,
then it started again,
I didn't want it to,
but it did,
again
and again
and again,
bringing it to an end,
I walked out,
and woke up.

Julia Coroama (12)
Highgate Wood Secondary School, London

PAINT

Her face is an empty, blank canvas,
just a blank space.
She believes it masks her femininity,
she feels just too much misplaced.

She grabs her brush, starts with the base,
she begins to feel more in place.
She applies it layer by layer, feeling more pretty,
bearing in mind no one will feel any pity.

Without her warpaint, she feels too defenceless,
weak and broken, she's completely powerless,
without this armour, she will crash and burn,
knowing one day these tables will never turn.

She begins to realise her canvas isn't the only problem,
but it's the stand beginning to collapse.
She changes her appetite with any excuse,
ignoring the fact it's just pure self-abuse.

People start to notice, people start to talk,
because everything she paints on can rub off like chalk.
Her canvas starts to tear and her stand begins to rust,
until her whole future turns into dust.

Emer Stevens (14)
Highgate Wood Secondary School, London

UNTITLED

You say so much to hurt me,
To cause pain to my soul,
To cause harm to my mind,
To cause scars and bruises to my body.
You say so much to upset me,
To make my eyes rain,
A rain that will never stop raining
And causes my heart so much pain.
You say, you shouldn't wear that skirt, it makes you look fat!
Well, if you really cared you wouldn't say that.
All you do is put me down,
Make me feel small, if you really loved me, you'd make me feel tall.
Taller than a mountain, more beautiful than the sea,
You don't really know me...
You know what you think, not what you see,
You see a presentable young lady, but you think she is a slut.
So you knock her down and tell her to give up.
Well, here's some news for you, I will stand my ground
And I will make everything I do count!
Your words don't affect me anymore, bully!
Clearly you're the one that needs help, not me.

Moresha Mariama Mansaray (13)
Highgate Wood Secondary School, London

BOOK POEM

It's just paper and ink,
Yet it's another world,
It's just paper and ink,
Yet it's an escape,
It's just paper and ink,
Yet it's the wildest dreams,
It's just paper and ink,
Yet it's a teleport to anywhere,
It's just paper and ink,
Yet it's magic,
It's just paper and ink,
Yet it can teach everything,
It's just paper and ink and if you let it,
It will take you beyond the rainbow.

Ella Phillips (13)
Highgate Wood Secondary School, London

LIFE'S PURPOSE

Some are lost, some yet still to find
The true purpose of their existence
They search in all the wrong places
As time goes by and the years wasted

Greed, wealth and power to name a few
Of man's enemies to man's true purpose
All distractions to man's eternal glee
As time goes by and the years wasted

Vanity, pride and lust, all indulgences
Of the flesh as man neglects his soul
Knowing not if tomorrow he shall see
As time goes by and the years wasted.

Najibah Batanda (11)
Highgate Wood Secondary School, London

NEW BEGINNINGS, BIG DREAMS

A fresh start, a new beginning,
Wonder why my head is spinning.
Walk away, no looking back,
Had a great time here, there's no doubt about that.
Put my hand in my pocket and pull out my report,
Done well in most subjects, even good at sport.
Had the best times here, that no one can deny,
But it's time to move on now, my chance to fly.

Highgate Wood, heard it's good, the uniform's not bad either.
Sure I'll be fine, have my big sister in Year 9
To help me out when I need her.
So onwards and upwards, that's what they say,
No matter what's ahead of me, I'll be sure to seize the day!

New beginnings, blue sky, I think I can fly,
My dreams will take me there.
Up, up and away, reaching higher each day,
In the skies on a wing and a prayer.

Aiming high, shooting for the sky,
Being the best me I can be.
Showing the world what I'm made of,
No holding back, I'll just take off,
There'll be no stopping me.

I've got what it takes, no need for breaks,
Got a fire in my belly, not just going to sit and watch telly.
Turning dreams into reality will give me
Some clarity, a happiness within.

Cream rises to the top, so don't ever stop,
To give up would be a sin.
The world's my oyster and I'm the pearl
No doubt about it, you'll remember this girl!

Kate Alexandra Jevons (12)
Highgate Wood Secondary School, London

NOTHING, NOTHING, NOTHING

Nothing but death,
Nothing but pain,
Nothing but grievance,
Like standing in rain.
Nothing to give,
Nothing to take,
Nothing to hear
When the whole world's at stake.
Nothing to do,
Nothing to be,
Nowhere to live
Try to act like you're free.
No one to love,
No one to care,
Just you alone
There's nobody there.
Nothing but death,
Nothing but pain,
Nothing but grievance,
Like standing in rain.

James Hastings O'Shea (11)
Highgate Wood Secondary School, London

CATS

All alike, yet so different,
Asleep or awake,
Big or small,
The being in my arms had feelings, emotions, thoughts,
Yet some treat it like a grain of sand on a beach,
Pointless, unnoticed, yet hungry for love.
They are scared of us, as we tower over them,
Menacing, threatening,
We know this world much better than them,
They are frightened, though they don't show it.

Eliza Buckton (11)
Highgate Wood Secondary School, London

WINTER'S NATURE

The blissful twilight fell across the land as the night commenced.
It shadowed the snow, leaving it dun.
All the summer animals hide away as hibernation has begun,
Muted sounds from all directions created a peaceful tune,
A stone feathered the surface of the lake that glistened under the luminous moon.

The soft breeze formed a spiral of silver snow,
Dancing along with the gentle motion of a willow.
Squirrels nestled, robins swooped and foxes played,
Their delicate footprints led through a glade.

The winter chorus played across the forest.
The winter stirred in the breezy air.
The winter freeze created icicles on branches.
The winter is a dream, not a nightmare.

Maya Muir (11)
Highgate Wood Secondary School, London

POETRY

The seagull, the beautiful bird.
Gliding through the lush, soft breeze,
the sunlight shone beautifully in the sky.
The bird flew around like a god to the Earth,
its feathers were the texture of cotton.
As it swooped down to the tip of the lake
its delicate wings opened up as it surfed over the lake.
The triumphant bird rose up
as the rest of the group started to leave.
Never will that majestic bird be forgotten.

Stan Webb (11)
Highgate Wood Secondary School, London

SMOKE

We're watching everything go up in flames,
We and our lives have burned bright,
Like a candle, but now we're standing alone,
In utter, devastating darkness. Have we been devastated?

Our candle burning so viciously and passionately, burned at both ends,
Our time was short, but oh we shone like a star...
But even stars burn out eventually.

Now we watch the smoke as it clouds our vision, our judgement,
The smoke a hazy devil, twisting and turning our beating hearts
To shrivelled, blackened stone, it's so cold without our glorious fire,
So cold the smoke rises, yet we fall like out empire of cards,
A house so delicate and fragile,
All it took was a breath, a sigh to destroy it all.
The ruins of what once was and will never be again,
Haunts us like ghosts and our freedom, happiness,
Our will to live will dissolve like

Smoke!

Ellie Hutchings (12)
Highgate Wood Secondary School, London

WHAT IS IT?

It awakens every morning hoping for the finest,
It expects disappointment and failure at the lowest of times.
Its cry for help can be heard from miles away,
But, when it obtains what it needs, it can rise above all others and exceed all expectations.

Their scars are the gateway to their mysterious past
But they only look up to the unknown future.

They dance to the point where their whole body is numb,
Their uniqueness is unlike any other traditional creature.
This being has many tales to tell,
but their confidence is overshadowed by anxiety.

They have dreams to perform, to dance, act, design,
inspire.

They know not to make the same devastating mistakes
as some who are close,
But they also know how to take delicate risks.

She is a powerful girl in her eyes, who believes in equality for *everyone.*
She will not allow the past to deteriorate her destiny.
She is me!

Yelena Jourdan-Wicker (11)
Highgate Wood Secondary School, London

HOPE

When your world is crumbling down
But you look up and it's rain
And your life is still standing
When you want to collapse because your heart can't hold its pieces together
But your legs are as strong as rocks
And your heart is still beating
When the cuts are opening once more
And your head is going to explode
But there is no blood running down your wrist
And your skull is still holding your thoughts
When you feel like you can't carry on
So you run far away
To feel like you're not alone
Because you think it's what you need
And the angels start coming down
To take you to that place after life
But you realise that it's the friend you can always trust
And she pulls you back to life
Holds you as you cry
That's when you realise
Realise you are not alone
She will always be there
When you need her most
She gives you hope
She gives you life
She's there when you want to say goodbye
But then will never let you,
Never let you say goodbye.

Amy Davis (13)
Highgate Wood Secondary School, London

HUMAN NATURE

When someone is hurting,
Do we see their fear;
Do we see their trembling fingers
And their flooding eyes?
Or do we see what we want to:
The plastered smile,
The crumbling lies?
Do we see their built-up wall slowly come crashing down?
Do we see their broken bones
From the pain they carry around?
Do we hear their silent calls as they sit there in the dark?
Do we see their bleeding soul, sunken eyes and broken heart?
Do we see their shattered pieces,
Scattered on the ground?
Do we pull them back together,
Or leave them all around?
And do we see we're all the same;
We hurt, we cry, we all have pain,
But we hide it from ourselves by building walls back up again.
We speak empty words,
Tell open lies,
Make broken promises, betrayed by our eyes.
Do we see it's not just you
Who ignores others while they ignore you too?
And there's the real problem,
There's nothing that we do;
Because if you want to help someone,
You have to start with you.

Tallulah Cox (12)
Highgate Wood Secondary School, London

BULLY

You are the bully who follows me by day,
You are the bully and that is not okay,
You are the bully who calls me names,
You are the bully and this isn't a game.

You are the bully who stops my sleep at night,
You are the bully convincing me to commit suicide,
You are the bully and this isn't funny,
You are the bully putting butterflies in my tummy.

I am the victim living in a nightmare,
I am the victim, my life just isn't fair,
I am the victim living life in fear,
I am the victim, I just want to disappear.

If you are getting bullied, stand up for yourself,
If you are the bystander, stand with everyone else,
Most importantly, never let bullies leave scars,
Because everyone in this world is perfect, just the way they are.

Maya Louise Kane (11)
Highgate Wood Secondary School, London

FEAR

Bullets ricocheting past my head
I was careful, watching where I tread
My heart thumping in my chest
I tried my best

I looked up to the sky
Letting each minute pass me by
Watching my back
I was starting to lose track

Most families lost someone dear
Only the end of the war would end all their fear.

Grace Heron (13)
Highgate Wood Secondary School, London

THE ADDICTION

I stare at it,
the obsession takes control of me,
I reach across my desk,
my only friend, never to be let out of my sight,
my only friend, never to let me down,
my faithful companion.

As I walk towards it,
it purrs at me, urging me to come closer,
drawing me in,
oh the beautiful, sweet sound of its tone.

I grasp the gorgeous object in my hand,
its gleaming, shiny newness winking at me,
its slim, smooth cover
my fingers wrap around it.

'Hello,' I say,
it speaks back to me.
'Hello, it's Siri here, what can I help you with?'
'A game, a map, another app,' I whisper back.
Twitter, Instagram, Facebook and feeds,
oh the many Internet needs.

I worship all these gods,
time and time again.
As each hour passes
I become more involved,
more at one with it,
without this object of desire
my life would never be on fire.

Until I spy another one,
an iPhone 6 or 7,
Obsession gone!

Manon Elliott (11)
Highgate Wood Secondary School, London

ON MY WAY

I am now in Year 7
Reminiscing about my previous heaven

It's been so hard in such a big place
When the buzzer goes it's a fast race

Students rush into long corridors
Without any time to stop and pause

Heavy bags flung over aching backs
No time to have long chats

Relentless stairs up and stairs down
People walking with a frown

When the buzzer goes it's a fast race
A sea of people moving around
Push, shove, nudge, no personal space
All set to a loud sound

All the people look the same
Lots of children, unknown names

Wearing nothing more than dreary blacks
Except for the coloured rucksacks

Heart beating, full of worry
Late children in a mad hurry

Noisy feet, chairs scratching
Doors slamming, teachers teaching

When the buzzer goes it's a fast race
A sea of people moving around
Push, shove, nudge, no personal space
All set to a loud sound.

Laurie Logue (12)
Highgate Wood Secondary School, London

UNTITLED

Roses are red, violets are blue, but some are black,
you see not everything and everyone is perfect.
Not everyone's lives are prim and rosy,
some people think that life is great and that you should live it.
But on the other hand, some people think that life is angry
and can't wait for it to be over.
This someone could be anyone.
It could be your milkman, it could be that person you walked by
in the corridor, it could be anyone.
Some people are more unlucky than you, and haven't been born into
a happy family, or a family which has got enough money to feed them,
this could be anyone.
Some people don't want to go home after the bell rings,
some people want to stay far away from their home,
this could be anyone.
So next time you bump into someone in the corridor
and you are going to push past them,
think about who you're pushing.
Because you might make their life that extra bit painful,
they might snap and try to kill themselves,
or they might lose their minds,
because not everyone's life is as perfect!

Paddy Newcombe (11)
Highgate Wood Secondary School, London

A STORM OF WAR

Swollen tears dropped from above,
sky was grey, stripped of love,
the wind howled and screamed,
it felt like something I had dreamed.
As a pale white dove soared across the sky,
our minds were cleared, to think of those who had to die.

Dani Weiss (13)
Highgate Wood Secondary School, London

UTOPIA

When I look out my window, all I can see is snow for miles and miles,
as if it is a blank page of unlimited possibility and the unknown.
If I could, I would write a perfect Utopia future on it,
with no dystopian aspects,
when I close my eyes I imagine myself in this Utopia,
I feel happy and excited, like a cat that just got a new toy,
because I'm the god in this world and no one can tell me to change
this Utopia or to change me.

There are trees dotting the surrounding atmosphere
blocking a way for the sun to leak through
and melting the unharmed, crystal-white snow,
but after all this is only a poem I'm writing in my bedroom,
because my mum's making me, so sorry to ruin your dreams,
all those little kids who believe this.

Alex Matthew (13)
Highgate Wood Secondary School, London

UNTITLED

I looked out of the broken window, the icy wind blowing into the empty room,
filled with sorrow from the world in front of me.
The ground covered with some kind of thick sheet of dust,
oppressing the life out of the city hiding below.
Looking down on it, I feel like I'm stuck somewhere I don't belong,
Nowhere to go, this is our world, the empty shell it is becoming,
I close my eyes, willing myself to find the memories if the smiles the love...
But it's now here to be found.
Overpowering these thoughts, my mind is filled with visions
of suffering, depression, resentment.
The desert lying before me is my home.
How we got here I don't know,
but it's where I belong.

Yasmin Walton (13)
Highgate Wood Secondary School, London

UNTITLED

Here is a pen with the world in the nib,
Draw the Earth
Make it your own.
Use the carriage to drag open day
and drag open night
Write your future
make it good
Don't add life without hearts
People with homes, heat and lives
not just people who live in a slum
As the clock ticks by, it's nearly ready
Ready to unveil your masterpiece
with everyone happy,
healthy and
with a great life.

Louise Roberts (12)
Highgate Wood Secondary School, London

BRIDPORT

Wind blows into my hair,
Air is cool,
Flying birds.
This is Bridport,
Coastal town.

Day has passed,
Sun is down
And moon is soaring
In Bridport's sky.

Birds can sing,
Woods may sway,
Its populace can walk
Kids may play
In grasslands by Bridport.

Faber Bell (13)
Highgate Wood Secondary School, London

UNTITLED

If a man kills a man,
Who dies that day?
You can hear a man screaming,
but can you hear his heart breaking?
Once a man is shot,
His soul soars above,
It's his big hands awakened.
The murderer waits to be taken,
The victim is still alive,
Remembered in people's minds,
But the murderer is dead,
He haunts the streets, he's full of dread.
There's a hole in his body,
That can never be fed,
It's the whole of his heart
Which slowly fills with meds.
It's the pills he's been taking,
To try and get out of his head,
But he can't escape and no one can penetrate,
As he lays there pondering,
He's wondering,
If his head will ever stop thundering.

Ruby Morgan (13)
Highgate Wood Secondary School, London

DAY

Night is a point during which most stay dormant
Night is a point during which nobody's around
Night is a point during which crowds occupy clubs
Night is a point during which roads stay still

Morning is a point during which toast is popular
Morning is a point during which morning frost falls
Morning is a point during which adults go to work
Morning is a point during which kids go to school

Noon is a point during which work stops
Noon is a point during which stomachs groan
Noon is a point during which chums catch up
Noon is a point during which to unwind

Sundown is a point during which to sit back and watch TV
Sundown is a point during which family laugh
Sundown is a point during which babas nod off
Sundown is a point during which to tidy for tomorrow

Night is a point during which most stay dormant
Night is a point during which nobody's around
Night is a point during which crowds occupy clubs
Night is a point during which roads stay still.

Joshua Kingston (12)
Highgate Wood Secondary School, London

INDIVIDUALITY

It's not fair,
It's not right,
It's not just
And it's not rational
To pick on,
Bully,
Fight,
Hurt
Or prohibit,
Just for not conforming with your opinion.
Allow individuality.
Honour Human rights.
Champion variation.

Flo Stroud (11)
Highgate Wood Secondary School, London

THE SUN

As I gape at the sun,
I wonder how beautiful and rigorous
An object can be, nothing could be outdone,
I lean closer and now realise it's so mysterious.
It feels like the sun spins around me, but now
it feels the opposite way round. I feel her glare
sting like thousands of scorpions, in a deadly pit,
my heartbeat barricades as she blasts a solar flare.
She laments in agony, a group of clouds crowd
onto her, halting her face like a peacock mask.
The clouds reign supreme, as they spread the
surface with no sunlight and no life, the
clouds attack with droplets of rain
slithering its way, only if
there was the sun.

Erden Gungor (13)
Highgate Wood Secondary School, London

THE GOLDEN BOOT

The passion that is stashed
inside the core of his soul.
When the lightning spark of his boot,
walloped and whisked at the ball,
his effort led its way towards the awaiting goal.
Its swift manoeuvre captures a thousand eyes,
which is caught in the practise of future minds.
The moment is encapsulated in soccer's history
by the cherished ideals of football glory.
Pele's refined finesse and Ronaldo's prowess as a footballer.
Maradona, *'The Golden Boy'*, with the dancing ball.
Messi, *'The Atomic Flea'*, whose spirit taught him to succeed.
The forever illuminated faces whose endeavours will never die.
How will you ever even try?
Tread inside the heart of football
and you will understand.
But when he wins a match,
why do tears appear.

Because football is not just a ball.

Hakeem Edwards (11)
Highgate Wood Secondary School, London

DARKNESS

Darkness is a room full of nothingness
A room full of smokiness
Why is this room full of woe?
What is this craziness?
Is there no way out of this excruciating pain?
Darkness surrounds me
I never knew there could be such an agonising ache
I endure these feelings of hopelessness
Darkness is a room full of nothingness
Darkness.

Tsiona Fernandes-Tadesse (12)
Highgate Wood Secondary School, London

THE POWERS OF LIFE

Our planet is amazing
creating new possibilities
but the world is still hiding
the doors to life.

Walking on Earth
swimming in the water
breathing the air
and roasting with the fire.

The four elements
are the keys to the doors
but can we really find them?
It's a mystery to all.

But we are still living
and we have a routine
and if you don't follow it
our world isn't supreme.

So you are asking me
what's the routine?
Well, let me tell you
but you might not be surprised.

Wake up and go to school
Come home and do your homework
do your chores
or you will be poor.

We have come to the end of our story
and even though our routine isn't supreme
life is still amazing
as we continue knowing.

Layla Badalova (11)
Highgate Wood Secondary School, London

THROUGH THE LOOKING GLASS

Here yet again,
Living through pain,
My teardrops stain,
I want to get hit by a train.

Come home from class,
Look into my glass,
Hate middle class,
Cos of every class I've passed.

Getting laughed at,
Spat at, fell flat,
Because of that,
I feel like I want to die.

Just say goodbye,
I want to cry,
Just had to try,
Look up to the midnight sky.

I prayed to God,
It might sound odd,
The firing squad,
The heart I had felt so clawed.

Sophia Doncheff (14)
Highgate Wood Secondary School, London

MY BIRTHDAY

I'm on the Tube, on the Victoria Line,
A fellow lady's handbag is constrained with mine,
The panels of light above,
Flicker, as I drink out of my mug.
I cling on to the polished, light blue pole,
That steadies me and makes me feel bold,
As the Tube comes dashing into the station,
A horde envelops me, but I am patient.

Carefully stepping onto the platform,
I suddenly get pushed and trampled on,
People come at me, barging and banging,
An unstoppable force sets my nerves twanging.

Taking a breath I exit onto the street,
As I emerge I feel a tremendous heat,
My ears tune into the sounds of what's around,
I start to hear engines and music quite loud,
Suddenly a wave of emptiness strikes me,
It's not crowded, nor is it busy.

I look around me at the abandoned street,
Wondering why people would flee,
Shops are left open,
Cars are broken,
Hurriedly walking into Marks and Spencer,
I notice that there is food left on the counter,
A sense of panic trips me up and I'm dazed,
Where is my friend on my important day?
I run out and into a pub,
There are glasses on tables, left half drunk,
Then I notice candlelight,
A birthday cake; I feel fright.

Victoria Stogdon-Culbert (13)
Highgate Wood Secondary School, London

LONELY

I waited, waited for it to stop,
to stop pouring rain and hatred from the sky,
I was forever stuck inside,
inside a place of no imagination,
yet forever sheltered from the weight of the world around me.

Trapped inside a cage of no emotion,
outside I'm surrounded by friends, but inside I'm all alone,
nothing can fill the black hole growing inside me,
hoping for someone to come with the key of the cage that confines me,
but only hoping and only waiting, a continuous cycle.

Always watching but never really there,
wanting to love but not able to feel,
surrounded by things I can't do, can't feel, can't see
and I am forced to watch people do all the things I can't do,
feel all the things I can't feel and see all the things I can't see.

Every night I look out my window
and find the world has moved again,
moved on without me
and every day it gets further and further away
and every day, I get further from the life I had,
while the world moves I am stuck in one place,
as If superglue is holding me down.

They say, just smile the bad things away,
but it's harder than it seems,
to me it's obvious, I'm hurting
and I can see when others are too,
but everyone else is oblivious to my pain,
oblivious to how I feel nothing.

Olivia Dennis (12)
Highgate Wood Secondary School, London

REMEMBER ME

Remember those times when we danced till dawn?
When you smiled, it gleamed in the sunset,
your fragile, elegant movements so dainty, so gentle and slow,
it made people wonder if you could be the sun just above the horizon,
rising to be our morning star.
Remember when twilight struck?
We used to sing those songs and melodies of the nightingales, so subtle, so soft,
your voice powerful, it made people wonder if you were of this world...
if you were an angel.
But do you remember me?
I remember the last time I saw you, fearful, pale and you didn't have that smile,
that beautiful gleaming smile,
your eyes usually are luscious green and full of life.
The key that beheld the universe was now dark and grey, full of a touch of guilt.
They had gone cold as you looked deep into my eyes,
my soul filled with darkness and depression,
shivers went down my back like the feeling you get before you vomit.
There were no more glowing eyes that were the key to my heart!
As your eyes filled with water, mine did too,
the tears that fell down your face, I felt them rolling through the creases
of my dry, rough skin.
I tried to speak, but not a word came out,
you fell slowly, like a feather, to the hard, cold ground.
I watch, trying to move, over and over again, as if demons were holding me down
to watch the traumatising sight.
I tried to help you, my brain started to fade, my mind went drifty,
my body went cold, I felt as if I was floating there so slowly,
above the meadows we used to play around, blurry and faint I heard your cries,

croaky and dry, my eyesight began to fade away,
my vision eventually became darker, my breaths became slow,
heavy and faded.
I stopped breathing, my eyes shut.
Remember me...

Shanya Braithwaite Ambrose (12)
Highgate Wood Secondary School, London

BIRTHDAYS

Today is my birthday
A Sunday in May
With music and food
I can't wait to play

Rock and roll drums
With guitar thrown in
Laughing and singing
A humungous din

Crunchy crisps and pizza
Biscuits and cola slush
Doughnuts, tarts and popcorn
What a sugar rush!

I got lots of gifts today
Books, films, socks and toys
All sorts of random stuff
Just right for girls and boys.

Felix Andrew (11)
Highgate Wood Secondary School, London

LIFE IS CORRUPT

Life is corrupt,
it will never let me win
and dreams are just dreams
which will never sing.

No matter what I do,
no matter how hard I try,
no one will hear
my passionate cries.

The world is engulfed by woeful conflict.
Life is a struggle on its own.
I'm hurt, but who cares,
I'm all alone.

Hey Life!
You weird creation,
your world is dying,
your world is crying
and what are you doing,
just waiting, solitary,
seldom hearing me.

You shatter dreams,
you disappoint
and as I hold onto the shards
you laugh and mock.
The blood on my hands,
bad blood, poison!
Vengeance, revenge,
Life, let me win!
Please...

My kindness does not work,
my strategy is failing,
jealousy is rising!
Hate comes from my heart!
Anger courses through my veins,
but lashing out is not the answer.

Crying won't solve anything,
Nothing will work.
Life is a jerk, Life is corrupt,
Life will always win
But I will never give in...

Ramneet Kaur Bains (13)
Highgate Wood Secondary School, London

THE NOT SO FORTUNATE WORLD

If only the world could stay bright,
Stay warm and happy through day and night.
Racism, sexism, the words of today,
The words that separate the straight and the gay.
You open the news, war is here and there,
Walk down the street, hurt, no one will care.
What has the world come to?
What is there left to do?
If only there was that spark,
The spark which led us through the dark.
Fighting for the rights just to live,
No man out there wants to give.
No one is perfect, everyone dies,
People hate the truth but sleep with lies.
It is a dream that African-Americans are free at last
And that discrimination would be a thing of the past.
These battles aren't easy and hard to fight,
We will be fine as long as we stand up for what's right.
We have to make sure that the world keeps its dreams alive,
That this world will carry on striving to thrive.
Women used to sit by, bullied by men,
But we're living now, not back then.
This is now the version of World's hell,
What have we come to? No one can tell.
Come together, unite as one,
Believe forever, forever to come.

Yasemin Ozalcin (13)
Highgate Wood Secondary School, London

SCHOOL

Oh school,
Six hours of your primary soul
wound up with your form tutor
filling your brain with rubbish!

Oh school,
What is going on
with short food hours
and that horrid, dinging thing
that brings lunch to a halt?

Oh school,
I carry a hunch that
it might not stay a horrid prison
that I obtain with my brain
and don't look forward to.

Oh school! You will do OK.

Sophie Gill (12)
Highgate Wood Secondary School, London

DUSK

Dusk falls and within I am,
Again I am, within thy dusk,
Waiting; but for what?
That is thy worry.

Stars, moon or our dawn's hurrah?
Why so I wait?
I am not dawn,
I am not dusk,
Just a solitary star in thy light.

Mimi Brown (12)
Highgate Wood Secondary School, London

POWER

Power is something we all want
It is something we crave and are greedy for.
People with power misuse it
People without power suffer.

Power, we all want it
All of us have it
But it makes us want more!

Yousaf Khan (12)
Highgate Wood Secondary School, London

UNTITLED

A bench that stands, not completely alone
is kept company by the deadly shadow -
the deadly shadow of something
stone cold
No one wants this company because it
is all just one misery
and blocks out the fun from old, enjoyable
activities.

No one dares to sit on this bench
for it's an empty space that wants
to dominate and surround.
We cannot feed this thing with our
feelings, we must accept and move on
otherwise it just keeps reeling.

Mia Blasi (13)
Highgate Wood Secondary School, London

A BEAR HUNT

The padding paws
The slashing claws
The biting teeth
A sword in it sheath
He wanders up without a care
Ready to kill the unsuspecting bear

He stands up to twice his height
The hunter gets a fright
The bear growls
The hunter prowls
And he squeezes the trigger tight

The beast is hurt, but not yet dead
The hunter runs back, back to his sled
The bear chases
The hunter's dumb
Because he was running to his mum

'Mum!' he cried, but it was too late
Because the bear had him served up on a plate!

Tom Roberts (14)
Highgate Wood Secondary School, London

PAINS OF LOSS

A sharp stab from an icy sword,
A constant rival within,
A cut that will not try to fix,
No scab, no scar, just a gaping wound.

It is a loss of a thing or a body that has amity of all our minds that authors this pain,
But that is not always so much of a load that it can tip bowls in many trials of days,
It is by a ticking clock of all things that starts and stops, that push us to pass away.

A hollow pit, a blank coat of rock,
Is what all wish to run from,
A box of wood falling into hard ground,
Dirt soon stops any looking at this box of astray souls.

Falling drops of salty liquid splash and sink into ground,
Night-black cloth that all must shroud in,
Song of a saint that casts lost souls away,
Cold winds of icy sorrow attack all.

Nothing has not known its wrath,
All run from it,
But nothing, not a soul, not a thing outruns it,
It haunts all, it hunts all, it at no point withdraws.

Katya Dickson (11)
Highgate Wood Secondary School, London

UNTITLED

I didn't know I was going
That's why I didn't warn you I wasn't coming back
I look at you and wish you didn't mourn
It's hard having to watch you sit at night and cry

I'm sorry for what I put you through
I can't think of how this is for you
Just know I'm sorry for abandoning you
And I'm waiting for you
But until that day, don't mourn my loss

I want you to know all my passion and joy has found its spot again
I'm in Zion and in Zion I'll stay

I admit it, loss isn't basic nor is it straightforward
So I wish my words of passion catch you prior to your fall
I want you to laugh with that glow again
I really want you to find comfort.

Zandile Mathebula-Jonah (13)
Highgate Wood Secondary School, London

NO TO WAR

No to war is what I say,
It's fun to watch kids laugh and play,
Don't want no bombings, confusions or dismay.

I pick school, gifts and food all day,
Guns and ammunition, no way, no way.

Nobody should cry, war brings pain,
Bring us joy with pouring rain.

Tranquillity and adoration brings us unity,
I don't want that ugly looking animosity.

Happy kids, so you I will pray,
Now, tomorrow or any coming day.

Don't want our fun to go away,
Don't want our joy to go astray.

Jenasia Walker (11)
Highgate Wood Secondary School, London

YOUTH

I put on a mask,
Mock a grin,
Bluff as if I'm strong,
Laugh,
Play along with it,
Say I'm okay.

But, in actual fact,
I'm crumbling down,
Crushing,
Hiding off pain,
Burying my soul,
Cloaking away agony.

As if I did admit it,
Quit lying
And finally said,
Okay,
I'm a youth,
From now on this is I.

I'm cool with it,
Against all odds,
I'm not solo,
A world of humans go though this,
I am strong,
I can carry on.

Selin Tas (13)
Highgate Wood Secondary School, London

SOCIETY

Many of us walk on this world
In various forms
Fat, slim, big, thin
Short, tall, giant, small
Humanity is fairly dissimilar
But in a way it's matching
All of us think, put up with pain
All of can support and aid
But individuals opt not to bind in chat
'I must dash,'
'I am busy,'
'Actually, I'm fairly dizzy,'
'No I cannot go,'
Humans must build trust
Stop judging unknowns for no good justification
Aim for altruistic traits
A day without arguing
A day without fights
A habitat with a tranquil night
Compassion had not hurt a soul
So show acts of good will in a world so cold.

Amy Tafliku (13)
Highgate Wood Secondary School, London

MY POEM

Pollution crushes our poor Earth every second,
We might not notice it, but most of the time it comes in second.
It might be just driving, it might be something more,
but never in first, our priorities before.
The Earth will be destroyed but it won't stop that,
neither will we, our unseeing eyes ever see.
Soon there will be nothing left of the world
it will be gone forever, no one or anything to see except silence,
furthermore, we will not see
millions of species.

Yet we end up being the ones to
demolish the world that was constructed to be perfect.
We built into the clouds for there is no room left on the ground.
We used it up, destroying people's homes
then building our own.

Evan Shute (11)
Highgate Wood Secondary School, London

WISDOM

Newborn's minds are very inconspicuous
Baby's brains are very discontinuous
Toddler's think tanks are very responsive
Children's brains on the other hand are very imaginative
Teenager's loaves are very boisterous
Middle-aged info cells can give you a surprise
Granny-bag's grey matter starts to get really wise
But it all doesn't really matter because at the end of the day your mind's shattered.

Rudi Wallis-O'Dowd (12)
Highgate Wood Secondary School, London

NIGHT

Softly and sadly
up on the hill
the bell
begins to toll.

Lock all the doors
blow out the light;
the hour is late
sleep comes with the night.

Close all the windows
smother the fire
sound slips into silence
when mortals retire

Downstairs is deserted
no one in the hall
sleep
rules over all

A day's work completed
now done the day
rest is now needed
for those made of clay

How soft is the night
where dark shadows fall,
sleep
captures us all.

Melissa Zara Kucuk (11)
Highgate Wood Secondary School, London

WHY IS IT ALWAYS MONDAY?

Why is it always Monday?
Why not always Fridays?
Monday is a grey cloud over my head
Friday is a fire-bursting ray of sunshine
Monday is a wave of depression
Friday is a bundle of joy rolling my way
Monday is around the corner ready to pounce
Friday is the light shining through
Monday is a headache drilling through your brain
Friday is resting your eyes for once
Monday is the devil underneath
Friday is the wings flying you away to happiness
Monday is your worst nightmare coming true
Friday is the fairy princess in your dreams
Monday is the haunted house dragging you in
Friday is the mansion with a great swimming pool inside
Monday is the pile of bricks cushioning your fall
Friday is a giant trampoline throwing you in the air
Monday is a fire, making you sweat a river
Friday is the warmness cuddling around you
Monday is the war tearing you apart
Friday is the peace making you smile
Monday is dropping your ice cream to splat on the floor
Friday is the sound of ice cream coming your way
Monday is the person that you hate
Friday is the person that you love
Why is it always Mondays?
Why not always the holidays?

Jessy Stoneman (12)
Highgate Wood Secondary School, London

COLD

Everything around me is growing cold.
A dark, black ice surrounds me
The frigid friendships once blazed a passionate vermilion
but now are dull, lifeless grey like my world,
it is a dull, lifeless colour, I am a dull, lifeless colour...
no sign of blue, because of the absence of red I shiver now.
I can see puffs of my breath, hot against this cold,
we're frozen over, all of us great glaciers
and icebergs drifting apart in the choppy sea that has existence,
sometimes I wonder *have I always been so breathtakingly alone?*

I've always been the type to stand in a crowd of strangers, family, friends and be completely alone, but sometimes the crooked smile and twisted fingers of utter, creeping loneliness pinches and pulls at the frays of my sanity.
I wonder how much longer can my stiff, cold fingers hold on?

Amara C.J Blair (12)
Highgate Wood Secondary School, London

LION

I used to be the king of the jungle,
High, much respected and well-renowned.
Helping, rummaging, teaching,
I was bold like a ferocious bulldog,
Stampeding, rampaging rapidly.
Hunting down my prey,
It finding difficult to hide.
It was a good life, a street free life,
I was a legend,
Everyone knew me.
Coming to me, bending down at my feet,
I was a thunderbolt.
My mane swiftly flowing in the wind,
I used to be the king of the jungle.

Sumayah Halder (12)
Islamia Girls' School, London

HEDWIG!

I departed from all places,
carrying my thick feathers.
I covered all those paths,
in all sorts of areas.

The Death Eaters did air attacks,
I proved in loyalty my worth.
I sacrificed at Harry's back,
then I departed from the Earth.

I still remember that wonderful day,
when I walked through platforms 3 over 4.
I still remember Harry's wonderful grin,
through Quidditch, chess and so much more.

Potter ran, walked, jumped then flew,
sometimes so high the broom said, 'Achoo!'
He let me hunt for juicy, squelchy mice at night,
bring it in his face and have a good piece.

For him I did in flight,
Carry messages for the good,
Throughout the realms of day and night,
Being all a true friend should!

I carried letter through day and night,
Harry Potter called me his companion,
Oh, oh! What a pleasant name.

If I'm Potter's companion,
I am probably special
And of course, essential...

I'm Hedwig!

Zainab Nawaz (11)
Islamia Girls' School, London

MY NIECE

She waved her arms wildly,
kicked out her legs like a raving bear,
spitting out her dummy in disgust at some terrible taste,
a roaring monster, an untamed animal.

She began to crawl, like a leopard learning,
then chatting non-stop like a bird's chorus,
her lips moved constantly,
then started to walk.

Without guilt she threw things like a crazy person, angry at enemies,
she sabotaged faces,
turning empathy into fraught stares.

Sometimes I do miss her
silly old ways,
a time lost but not forgotten.

Maryam Zeeshan (12)
Islamia Girls' School, London

THE WIND

On a summer's day I gently blow,
Swaying the treetops like they are dancing,
Blowing through the trees,
I can cause destruction wherever I go,
Windows smashing,
Trees falling,
When I am angry, I form a tornado,
Running through fields like sheep
Causing umbrellas to fly.

I blow the leaves off the trees,
They fly away with my breeze,
The leaves are rustling,
The sun is shining.

Zaynah Rashid (12)
Islamia Girls' School, London

THE AMAZON

I remember the lovely times I used to have
Using my branches to provide homes for birds and apes
I remember the days when the wind would envelop me
The strange looking tree frogs stretched on my tree trunk
I ruled from on high
Life was like heaven
It was a time I will never forget
The time before cutters came
That day was alarming
Paper was what they wanted
My world disintegrated
Into menus, books and loo rolls
Everything went, my friends and my habitat
Lost, unnoticed, *dead*
That's my world.

Mahek Nadeem (11)
Islamia Girls' School, London

THE POETRY TRIALS - LONDON AND MIDDLESEX

THE OLD KIDS

The kids were fit,
they used to run around in the grass,
exercise across the field,
energetically running around the coast,
rant, run, race in the gyms,
play tennis as swiftly as a bird,
their legs were angel legs,
but that was then, this is now.

all they do now is sit and watch,
this is what their lives have become.
They find more interest in fixing the Internet,
running around the coast, doesn't even cross minds,
all we hear from then now is the sound of their fingers touching screens,
there is no hope left.

Dilara Duran (11)
Islamia Girls' School, London

A NEW ADVENTURE

Rushing wildly, furiously and intensely
breathing like a lion ready to pounce.
People surrounding me,
laughing and chattering,
I remember when I could be them.
But things have turned,
upside down,
a cursed life, a joyous one.
Looking at me up and down,
flustered by the sight of my owl
Hedwig,
who is my mail man.
My long, dark, misty robes
which I treasure like gold.
Then it came in sight,
platform nine and ten!
I clamp my eyes shut, tightly
the wind slapping my face as if it's angry with me.
I take a deep breath like inhaling for my life
and run rapidly forward.
Now, from here on
my adventure begins
at Hogwarts,
I, the famous Harry Potter.

Manaahil Ahmad (11)
Islamia Girls' School, London

RUNNING THE RACE

Pounding, my heart tries to escape the
cage of my ribs, my chest heaves,
breaths stab painfully from within the
deepest recesses of the lungs,
yet the course lies before me
as it does behind me.
I run.
Legs and arms working furiously, like
spiders rapidly rushing down the web.
trying to keep up with my rivals, or
at least stay abreast of them.
Five right ahead of me,
Four beyond.
I'm in front of the other eight.

Halfway through now,
I still have some strength
stored for my sprint,
quickly, swiftly, dynamically,
I power forward like a rocket,
I pass one, then another two, again
another three, then the seventh, eight and
the ninth.
I can see it.
The cheers ring in my ears,
the day is mine,
the sun smiles upon my joy,
I have won!

Sarah Khawaja (11)
Islamia Girls' School, London

THE SAD LIFE OF THE STREAM

I remember long ago,
when I used to shine on sunny days,
but now it has all changed.
I used to play with Nature
and was its best friend,
We would laugh and chatter like the world would never end.
I would race the wind across the valley,
and would act as a play area for fish.
I stretched and danced on beautiful days,
people threw in shiny, bronze, silver and gold pennies
and I would grant their wish!
It was a dream come true, then it faded.
It was a time before factories and cars,
they acted like greedy children
and took up all the space,
filling the air with pollution
and left me suffocating in the shadows.
I sit still every day and night
and watch the sky turn dark to light.
I am restless and alone,
if you try to find me
you won't succeed.
Just go home.

Parisay Mirza Safdar (12)
Islamia Girls' School, London

MY LIFE

I remember when my life was perfect,
I danced in the cool breeze and
I bathed in the sun,
I shaded children as they played beneath me.

I remember the birds making nests on my rough, brown arms,
I remember the squirrels tickling me inside when leaving their
acorns as they hibernated for winter.

Until *they* came...
Killing my friends with chainsaws, with axes and blades.

I heard the screaming, crying and whimpering of my friends
as they were slowly dying, one by one.

And one day they had killed me
I am just a stump now, people jump on me, sit on me
and kick me, no one respects me.

I am just there, standing there, my glorious past
fading away, the breeze hitting me like a
tidal wave, I am no use anymore.

Aisha Fazil (12)
Islamia Girls' School, London

THE 'WICK' GARDEN

I remember when my life changed,
I stayed shut up, behind walls,
covered with roses, vines and leaves,
all my skin wintry brown,
my arms draped in beauty,
Like a silk shawl of white.
My arms thin, grey and brown,
Look like a sort of hazy mantle
Spreading over everything.
It was a dull time; a gone time,
A time before I grew.
Bud by bud, each delicate scented bud,
I grew...
My door creaked open after ten years,
a rosy-cheeked face poked in - looking,
massaging my skin.
Turning grey and brown to green,
a green veil hung
as the colour crept in.
Birds, fighting for spaces,
were my old friends.
Leaves uncurling and nice smells hung in the air,
Daffodils, snowdrops and lilies
bring glorious colour to me.
Golden trumpets are heard
as spring has arrived!

Hiba Ajwat Ul-Hasan (12)
Islamia Girls' School, London

THE WATERFALL'S STORY!

I remember when life was virtuous,
When I could hear water fall like music, washing smoothly over me,
When I could feel water gently surrounding me.
I was tall and monumental
like Big Ben!
People watched purple lilies flow over me
I was famous,
cameras snapping and flashing
My friends were lovely people
Fish, birds and plants were my visitors,
but now all I do is hate
Not my friends, they're endearing
little creatures.
The people, the nasty people
who took my place from me.
Now I'm no one,
the malicious builders broke me
into half and then I dried up
and left drops of water flow!
I have no one in this corrupted world,
I'm finished!
I don't have a wonderful life anymore.

Malaika Kashif (12)
Islamia Girls' School, London

THE STEALTH

I looked at it,
I ran up to it,
My arms swayed and swashed in a cruel wind.
Like a sheet on washing line,
The red and blue monster
There, in front of my eyes!
I sat restlessly in the seat,
The traffic light winked red,
Then yellow.
Everyone raised their phones like something great
Was about to happen.
Green lights up!
Oh no! Missed the photo!
We were twirling, swirling, swinging,
I hit my chin,
Banged my head,
Broke my tooth,
Dislocated my jaw.
I screamed
As we went upside down,
I came off the ride,
People in the sky,
Clouds on the ground,
That's right, I'm dizzy.
All because of The Stealth
At Thorpe Park.

Husna Hussain (12)
Islamia Girls' School, London

A BUTTERFLY'S STORY

I remember
Flying across the empty meadows
sitting on the apple tree leaves.
Then I flap my wings and fly to the wavy water
and spread leisurely on the scorching sand.
Then rest on the emerald-green grass
while I listen to the birds singing.
Suddenly a storm arrives,
it looks like a big, muddy puddle in the sky.
Dropping its anger across the land
it sprinkles its water on me.
The squirrels run rapidly back to the bushes,
as if there is a party to go to.
The birds fly back to the trees,
whilst I feel lost and frightened
and empty.
I need to hide...

Hanin Hasib (11)
Islamia Girls' School, London

THE RACE

I remember that intense
the sound of the extremely large man shouting, 'Get ready!'
My heart was beating as fast as Usain Bolt sprinting to the finish line.
As the whistle blew, I ran as fast as my legs could carry me.
The roaring of the crowd made my heart beat faster and faster.
As I was approaching the halfway line, my legs began to give way,
I could feel sweat dripping own my face as I approached the water table.
The thirst got the better of me as the finish seemed so far away,
I could see the trail of chicken feathers from the mascot in front of me.
Before I knew it, I crossed the finish line in second place.

Manal Elgiathi (12)
Islamia Girls' School, London

WE SPEAK OF REVOLUTION

We speak of revolution
like the kings of old
our heart a bitter cold

We speak of dreams
not to hear our child's screams
for the day we must fight
for the animals' right

O' the harness that lay
upon our backs no more shall pay
they shall drop on the ground
in triumph of our round

We shall see the morning come
in a sweet slum
we sleep, not to be burdened by the
sudden wake up
to work and work and work

We speak of revolution
to break free of the chains of humans
to do as we please
to not be looked at with displease.

Loiena Emmett (14)
Portland Place School, London

DIVINE DREAMING

Revolution
I thought of a world
Where our thoughts weren't curled
In spirals and spirals of news going viral
Where you and me
Were forever free
Of this silent oppression
Wrapped with discretion
I thought of a world with love and not hate
Where innocent people weren't prisoners of the state
Where women could walk all alone in the night
And the smiles of our children forever shone bright
Countries weren't bombed every day
And every child for his education could pay
I ask you now to hold my hand
Because in my mind I have a plan
You and I will create a revolution
As for this world that's the only solution
Hold my hand and hold it tight
We are changing the world tonight!

Lia Mordezki (13)
Portland Place School, London

WE KNOW IT'S TIME FOR A REVOLUTION

Children are dying and you just sit there,
there are hundreds of people running out of air,
they're running and you don't care.

You sit there in your almighty chair,
hiding in your evil lair,
while you see the Eastern world exploding and you just stare
because you don't care.

You let the children kill but don't want them voting
and when you see their bodies floating
all you care about is promoting.

You will give a kid a gun
and tell him to run
and just because he does not look like you
you tell him he is free to do
then he runs and he does not look back
and just 'cause he's black you shoot him in the back.

And then their heart forgets to beat
they might think that revenge is sweet
but they have nothing to eat
so they will always feel defeat.

The children have their dreams
of a life that gleams
however, this dies as they watch their mother float downstream
and you don't care
because you weren't there.

You talk to the children like they don't understand
telling them you're creating a wonderland
but this ain't happening with all the pollution
we know it's time for a revolution.

Oona Wolseley (13)
Portland Place School, London

REVOLUTION

Humanity, since the beginning of our existence
Has had failure after failure
We are left with our last country
Why has Humanity failed?

It is due to hierarchy?
Is it because we are the weakest?
Is it because we have weaker technology?
Does this mean we are fated to lose?

No, all of those are wrong
The reason we are able to live
To fight and survive...
Is because we are weak!

Because of our weakness we are strong
We trained our eyes, ears and minds
That is our trait as humans
Our trait is the ability of wisdom.

Because we are weak we learn and gain experiences
Rejoice! We are humans and we are talented
We are the most talented people
We were born without ability so we can achieve anything
This is the will of the weakest race.

Louis Chalupa (14)
Portland Place School, London

REVOLUTION

We are suppressed by people who don't really care
And if we speak our mind, they say, 'Don't you dare!'
We've picked them for something they promised to us
But now they're in power, they don't make a fuss

Blind faith will not lead us anywhere brothers and sisters
We need to teach a lesson to all those misters
If you think one person won't make a big change
Look at Martin Luther King,
He got people's lives rearranged

So I say revolt and take a stand
So your sons and daughters will live in a good land
The answer to this is a revolution
It was and will be the only solution.

Katy Khoroshkovska (14)
Portland Place School, London

SOUND POEM

The wind howled loudly to its own melody,
As the leaves endlessly rustled below her feet.
They matched together perfectly.
They made their own beat.

Thunder roared, lightning struck,
But she kept on running.
Rain tapped, clouds cracked,
But she kept on moving.

Ichhhca Rai (12)
Queensmead School, London

THE GIRL AT THE BACK OF THE CLASSROOM

The teacher's voice fades slowly away
As she sits in silence, time ticks by.
Childish chatter can be heard all around her,
Whilst she daydreams, nobody asks why,
Why, she sits at the back of the classroom.

Her dreams take her to distant lands,
Where trees loom over her, up above,
The sea is the sky and sky is the sea,
Nothing is as it appears to be,
When she sits at the back of the classroom.

The lesson continues without her knowing,
But in her head the trees they are growing,
As tall as the building she is in,
She doesn't take in the noise that surrounds her
Whenever she sits at the back of the classroom.

Her lesson is over, the bell is ringing,
The noise gets louder, break time beginning,
Trees fade away, the imaginary land forgotten,
The sea is not the sky, the sky is not the sea
Everything in this world is what it's supposed to be,

As she walks out of the classroom, her teacher wonders why,
Why she sits at the back of the classroom.

Grace Wells (14)
Queensmead School, London

NEVER TAKE PEOPLE FOR GRANTED

Her sweet face, her sweet white frosty hair,
She had a curing smile, it's just not fair.
She taught me how to write, knit, sing and read,
She was a good person she did a deed.
She will smother you with thoughtfulness,
In our lives she brought us joyfulness.

Please can you just stop, think and appreciate,
That they are your family, not your playmate.

Suddenly she was in hospital,
Immediately I felt so little.
Every day I gave her a sweet kiss,
Chocolate cures everything, but doesn't cure this.
The clock synchronised her heartbeat,
Slowing down as I sit in this seat.

Please can you just stop, think and appreciate,
That they are your family, not your playmate.

I stood in front of everyone and said,
A nice poem, I wish she wasn't dead.
I choose to be thankful and not sad,
For all the wonderful years we had.
I stand by your rose and shed a tear,
I'll always be grateful because you were here.
I know that she is watching us from Heavens above,
There is nothing that I miss more than your love.

Please can you just stop, think and appreciate,
That they are your family, not your playmate.

So stop always having silly fights,
Because they might not live many nights.
So just be nice, helpful and really kind,
Don't let your loved ones out of your mind.

Grace Emily Ridgeway (12)
Queensmead School, London

WALKING UPON THE EARTH

I was walking upon the earth,
a place streaming with precious birth,
sweet-scented daisies swaying across,
leaden across, hoof printed dirt.

As the warmth departs with light,
comes darkness ready to bite,
hovering above the ancient oak,
gloats the owl into the deep merciless night.

Trembling, I trudge down the mossy path,
companions of mine are creatures of dark,
the cricket the charcoal, the great grey slug,
reminding each other to beware of the unforeseen bark...

In a blink, the track changed it's course,
down came my burden full of remorse,
with speed yet pride I glide along... *Thud!*
Where have I ended? A river of course.

Syed Hamza Hasan (13)
Queensmead School, London

NANDO'S

There is nothing as delightful as Nando's.
Those who disagree are such saddos.
Never have I ever seen such an attractive sight.
These chefs must have used all their might.
Oh Nando's, what food you have created.
Oh for so long have I waited.
You bring me joy, my dear Nando's.
Remind me of the poems Mary Angelou.

Narmin Safi (12)
Queensmead School, London

GOODBYE

There is nothing so beautiful as she
never have I seen a sight so perfect
though her wrath is a painful sting of a bee
her gorgeousness a crime, she a suspect
she has the attention of every he
her skin so smooth, not a single defect
she walks around absolutely carefree
her charm so strong you will fall for her too
her beauty so plain, like a landscape tree
as you say goodbye she waves her tissue
perfection, every single man should see
I look towards her blue eyes
will I see this beauty again?
Goodbye.

Abigail Bunker (12)
Queensmead School, London

BLACK LIGHT

I am the light to your dark
Yet you do not see me,
I stand alone and stark
You leave me lonely.

I watch you come and go
With in many moods
Sadness, Woe; Despair
I'm always there; so be aware

When I die you ignore
So in your memory I store
The glow of my small head
The next time you walk by me
Treat me as I were alive, not dead
So I can sleep merrily.

Levi Yeo (12)
Queensmead School, London

WI-FI

There's nothing more amazing than Wi-Fi
It's so perfect it is my dearest friend
I love you Wi-Fi, you're so strong and quick
We will be together until the end
You are so sacred like a baby chick
You're so fine, so nice, so compact, so sleek
You are worth every penny and pound
So divine you should be sold in a boutique
So clever you don't even make a sound
We won't betray you, you're part of the home
Although I can't see you, you are my love
You make it so swift to Internet roam
You are so modern, like rockets above
You will always have a place in my heart.

Rianna Christine Endersby (13)
Queensmead School, London

BIRDS CHIRPING

Birds chirping in the trees,
Singing of peace and serenity,
Whoosh, like the ocean breeze,
Soothing and cooling to the skin.

Sun-kissed tanning,
A bronze colour that gleams so bright,
Gleams like the sun rays,
Lights on a page, what a wonderful sight!

The importance of its meaning,
To listen is to learn, to learn is to listen,
Tunes in a bird chirping!

Parkavi Gnanasundaram (13)
Queensmead School, London

PAC-MAN

There is nothing so beautiful as Pac-Man,
Eating the pellets all day long,
I would play Pac-Man instead of pong,
Also I am your biggest fan.

Whenever I see you,
I think you are the best,
And that nothing else can contest,
Eating that cherry you cannot be blue.

When the ghosts come out to play,
you might have to sprint and run,
That's when they start to have fun,
Blinky, Pinky, Inky and Clyde

Pac-Man you are the best around
Nothing can beat that nom nom sound.

Ryan Silver (12)
Queensmead School, London

HAWAII

There is nothing so elegant as Hawaiian land,
Endless heartbeats drifting out to sea,
Volcanic temper as loud as a rock band,
But once you're there you feel so free.

Hidden amongst waters of the Pacific Ocean,
Enchanting fish using its beauty,
As important as Newton's second law of motion,
By creating Hawaii, God fulfilled His duty.

A sight so touching it brings tears to your eyes,
Adults smiling; children playing,
Hawaii is really the real prize,
That's what the entire world is saying.

The truth is crystal clear,
There is no place I'd rather be than here!

Meghana Trivedi (12)
Queensmead School, London

THE BEACH

There's no better destination to spend a vacation,
Than in a golden valley of relaxation!
Where the lush, green palm trees sway,
And the joyous children play.
The energetic colours of the reef glisten,
Whilst I gaze in utmost bliss trying to listen.
Intricate shells sit with vibrancy and fragility.
And the blinding sun sinks down with tranquillity.

Perambulating across the endless dunes,
Encompassed by utter emptiness.
Haunted by the deafening silence of isolation,
And startled by the ricocheting tides.
Not a single gull in the sky left,
As the gritty sand scrapes my feet.
I look for signs of life and company,
Yet nothing but barnacles remain.

Sahil Patel
Queensmead School, London

UNTITLED

Your beauty is unrivalled by anyone,
your smooth tones of blue and green,
reflecting the setting sun,
many wonderful mysteries, unsolved and unseen...

Sleep silently in your depths,
and many wrecks have now settled in,
the sailors that sank, said with their last breaths,
'Goodbye, forgive my sins.'

For all their lives they sailed the seas,
and saw many wonders,
they could never resist the ocean breeze,
but they got lost in your plunders...

As for me, the thing I hold dear,
in my fleshy hand,
is the ocean's kindest tear,
collected from the sand.

Lukas Serapinas (12)
Queensmead School, London

WHITE, WHITE

White, white is all I see,
in the mists of the diminutive droplets of ice.
As I ascend and embark on this adventurous mission of mine.
Every so often I am slapped by the passing wind, reminding me I am not numb completely.
The orange ball in the sky is now a distant memory.
The sweet smell of the summit, fills my nostrils nevertheless,
oxygen makes its way down,
it sends shivers down my feeble spine.
On the last few steps nature gives me its harshest.
However I overcome the challenges.
As my foot rests on the crisp snow,
I am overwhelmed with joy at conquering this Mars-like phenomenon.
I jump with glee!
Mesmerised with the sight of the never-ending white blankets.
The captivating sight blocks out the barbaric blizzard,
the sudden deafening silence alarms me.
The peak's drugs stops me from exhaling.
I find myself gawking in astonishment.
White, white is all I can see,
in the mists of the diminutive droplets of ice.
As I descend to spread the word of this adventurous mission of mine.

Nurany Sawda Khan (12)
Queensmead School, London

INTO THE WOODS

As I venture into the woods,
It gives me such a fright.
But when I open my eyes,
The sound of nature fills the night.
Water sparkles under a full moon's light,
A babbling brook drifts lazily by.
On its bank the crickets cry,
The aroma of summer is in the air.
Birds chirp without a care.
Snails slack upon a log,
Fireflies playfully tease a frog.
Leaves rustle in the gentle breeze,
Below hangs a hive of slumbering bees.
Daffodils lay beneath the trees,
Fluttering and dancing in the breeze.
A black and white raccoon catches a fish,
I hope I can stay forever, that would be my wish.

Zaheera Ghani (13)
Queensmead School, London

GUNSHOT

Gunshot fired through the sky,
Mouldy corpses scattered across the field,
People shout, 'C'mon boys, push it!'
Tiger! Tiger! The Germans bring out the big guns,
Smoke covers the picture until 20 men pass away,
They're on the sun still fighting for us,
My brother, you're brave but don't stop running,
You're the hero now,
Remember the saying: Dulce et decorum,
Est pro patria mori.

Jack Penny (12)
Queensmead School, London

A SONNET ABOUT HOPE

Happiness - it's a lost faraway land.
Laughter seems like an extinct emotion.
And all other feelings - they are just bland.
The ingredients to life - the potion
Became oblivious - causing some strife.
Full of sorrow Mother Nature departs.
Her tears as deadly as a pointy knife.
Life seems impossible - the brightest hearts
Turning stony - everything is in vain!
Suddenly the dull clouds part to reveal
Rays of sunshine glimmering through the rain.
A young girl - a butterfly surreal.
Smiling I realise hope will remain
Forever more in my treasured Ukraine!

Nataliya Klymko
Queensmead School, London

THE UNIVERSE

U nder the sun lies the world
N umerous things glory it in whole
I ce, liquids, solids too
V ery clever technology invented by men who
E very single one of us follow their influence, we should
R emember their intelligence, overrun us they could
S ound, sight, touch, smell, were given to us,
E very time you think, remember there is more behind its flow.

Yanky Deblinger (13)
Talmud Torah Tiferes Shlomoh, London

LONDON

London is a rainy city,
not to visit is a pity.
Transport by boat, bus or train,
you might want to stay in though, thanks to the rain.
To watch the guards changing, all tourists go
and down its famous canals you might want to row.
To an aquarium you can also go
and watch fish swimming to and fro.
Go to a giant toy shop in town,
So that no kids should go back with a frown.

Shimmy Grunfeld (13)
Talmud Torah Tiferes Shlomoh, London

WINE

D o you know of the excellent drink?
R ich in condition
I think it's very good
N othing could be better than it, it is
K ing of the drinks

W hite or red
I hold it is the best drink
N o, you don't hold like me
E very wine is known for being excellent.

Mordche Grosz (13)
Talmud Torah Tiferes Shlomoh, London

THE FUTURE

When will it be
Is it now? Tomorrow?
Will there be self-driving vehicles?
Robots occupying people's jobs?
Who will preside over the US?
Clinton, Trump, Rubio, to identify some,
Is there life beyond our world?

Mendy Hus (13)
Talmud Torah Tiferes Shlomoh, London

INVICTUS

(Before William Conquered England)

March my men into foreign lands
Row the ships until she reaches the sands
Autumn is slowly closing her book
Winter awakening to take a look
March under the two lions
Hark! Can you see the island?
The keeper is dead and the inn is open
And we march on until one has stolen
The golden prize. Brothers, don't be scared
We have tirelessly waited and prepared
For this day, this day will be our day!
We will march into the glory sun
Left our mothers and had our prayers done
For Father, for Brother and for King
Do you see the glowing light?
Do you hear the holy bells ring?
Dieu, verser votre lumiere sur nous
Sous votre gouvernance, nous serons
Invictus.

Morsal Safi Sarajzada (17)
The Ellen Wilkinson School For Girls, London

PERFECT

Being a teenager in today's society isn't easy.
You see all those models and celebrities photoshopped.
They spend five hours on hair and make-up and you compare yourself to them.
And you wonder, will I ever be like them?
You see them with their perfect hair, perfect skin, perfect body and perfect eyebrows.
They look flawless.
And you don't.
I've come to the point where I've realised beauty doesn't define
Who you are and that nobody's perfect.
I've accepted me for me.
And everyone else should.

Amy Pham (13)
The John Roan School, London

GAME POEM

Hackers are bad or are they?
I'm a gamer, fifty million subscribers,
Headshots everywhere,
So many views on YouTube,
That's what I'm about.
I'm the best now,
Everyone knows that I'm a
MLG Pro!

Rael Lutaj (11)
The John Roan School, London

NO HOPE, NO JOY

It should be about her,
But no.
It's about them,
Him and her.
The spotlight is on them.
Whilst she's there
In the corner.
Questioning her life.
Why?
Crying herself to sleep,
Every night.
Crying as she looks in the mirror.
Wishing to be that girl,
Wishing to be normal,
To be popular.
She has no hope,
No joy.

Cindy Nguyen (13)
The John Roan School, London

IF LOVE IS ENDLESS

If their love is endless,
Then there won't be any fights,
Fights that would lighten life,
If you feel for each other,
Then you'd look to the stars,
And take a wish for greatness,
Which will be given to you.
When the love is endless,
All this point it's the strongest,
But you'll only find that out once it's too late.

Nathan Biddlecombe-Nicolle (15)
The John Roan School, London

END OF THE WORLD WILL SOON COME

The world could end right now,
Right here where you are,
Can you imagine that?
You're doing something fun but that ends
Because of the biggest earthquake,
Or even the sun coming too far down,
If I was you just get prepared,
How about a bucket list?
Do everything before the world ends,
We all know it's going to end,
Sooner or later, get prepared,
The world will end, the world will end,
And you know it will,
We will be gone,
Everyone will be gone.

Debor Adams (12)
The John Roan School, London

THE WASTELAND

Grey skies rip across the atmosphere,
Darkness crushes the sun as the last sights of the city are viewed.
Cold, damp and ashes.
I am a pawn and the wasteland is the whole set, an opposition, an animal itself,
And its instincts are to kill, hunt but never to stop.
The vengeance and guilt of when it happened are the only reason I am still alive.
But when I reach the end,
I will become more powerful than everyone else playing the game.

Kai Sen (12)
The John Roan School, London

MEMORIES!

Memories, oh memory,
They're nice to remember!
When you're in a bad mood
Think back, remember
The greatest memory you would like to remember.
Either good or bad,
Past or present,
Late at night or early in the morning
Have a think!

Memories, oh memories
You're the greatest gift
You could possibly be the first on my list!
I'd rather sit down,
For a minute or two
And think about my memories,
The greatest of a few.

You could get back up,
Stay strong too,
If you try to remember your memories, or hopes,
You can feel emotionally free

Memories, memories
Memories, oh memories
They're nice to remember.

Titiana Varca (11)
The John Roan School, London

WHAT DOES THE FUTURE HOLD?

How will we ever know?
What does the future hold?
Will we share a common foe?
Another ice age, a land of cold,

Will the world be flooded?
Or an endless desert of heat?
Will we all be studded,
With an air of grim defeat,

Will aliens take over the Earth?
An end to a final battle,
Will they remember us, for all our worth?
Or will our fossils be mixed up with cattle?

Will all wars finally be stopped?
A step towards eternal calm,
With all our deathly fears be dropped?
Or will the world be like Animal Farm?

Dictators cannot control us all,
No matter of their power,
United, we will let none fall,
Even in our darkest hour,

The world cannot get any worse,
Than how it is today.
It's like a balloon, about to burst!
More than I can say.

James Keating (12)
The John Roan School, London

THINGS GET BETTER

Pain and mistakes are turning points,
I'll keep on moving if I break my joints.
Always stay strong and don't ever cry,
I'll never ever fail to try.

Get knocked down and rise back up,
Drown all my sorrows in a cup.
Keep on staying positive,
Never take but always give.

You won't really see,
But life's hard for me.
You should be who you are,
And keep smiling like a star.

Chloe Tu (13)
The John Roan School, London

DEEP IN THE OCEAN

Deep in the ocean,
As the fish swam through the waves,
The coral reefs grew,
Day by day.

Toxic waste falling,
Deeper and deeper,
The life in the sea,
Is getting weaker and weaker.

Sharks come to hunt,
Planning their traps,
Fish swim and hide,
And try not to get snapped.

The sun comes up,
The ocean springs to life,
Though other fish still go through,
Their struggle and strife.

Sulayman Ahmad-MacKinnon (13)
The John Roan School, London

MEMORIAL TREE

A soldier stands atop the hill,
The gun nestled in his arm,
Watching as his comrades fight on the barren battlefield.
No greenery for miles and miles,
Death's stench in every living thing.
He touched the acorn in his pocket,
A good luck charm from home,
And thought of the beautiful countryside of Kent.
He heard a *bang*,
He saw a flash,
He felt the blinding pain.
His body crumpled to the ground,
And Death came to make his claim.
The acorn slipped out of his hand,
And was ground into the mud,
Where it spent many a month shrouded in the darkness of the earth.
Slowly, as the years went by,
The acorn grew and grew,
Until that unlucky charm became an unlucky tree.
Limbs twisted as though in pain,
Branches gnarled and bare of leaves,
Roots tearing through the ground,
And through the bones beneath.
But it was the only tree for miles around,
And marked the battleground,
So it even got a name.
The monster that grew out of the acorn,
Became known as Memorial Tree.

Tallulah Millman (12)
The John Roan School, London

UNTITLED

As the sun comes up,
On this Saturday morning,
The hype about this sport is growing
Fans are coming,
From far away
To see their favourite team play
Two different colours,
At opposite ends,
Take their seats
To watch their side defend
The whistle blows,
The ball is kicked,
Who is first to score on the pitch?
The crowd is roaring,
The ball is in the net!
A shiny trophy, that team will get
As the two colours go home,
One happy, one sad
It will be next Saturday morning,
Till' a game there'll all be glad.

Charlie Sharpe (11)
The John Roan School, London

OH SWEET KORMA

Tick-tock, tick-tock I stare at the clock,
Waiting for the bell to herald that smell.
Oh silver pot, show me what you got,
With your colour of gold and flavour so bold.
My tongue comes to life with your sensational spice.
The sound of your name makes my brain go insane, oh korma.

Thomas Pratten (12)
The John Roan School, London

THE POETRY TRIALS - LONDON AND MIDDLESEX

THE CHRISTMAS TRUCE OF 1914

Bombed to bits by the German Fritz,
Tommies wounded by colossal bombs,
Machine guns spitting out rounds of bullets,
Bodies sadly splattered round the field,
As if the bombing would never end,
All for the sake of war!

But out pops a Christmas tree, from the Fritz side,
Serene, star-like shells fading in the morning sky,
Soldiers sweetly singing Christmas carols.
Then a German marches over, but he's unarmed,
The brave British Tommies are suddenly calmed,
All for the sake of war!

Tommies and Fritz play hundreds-a-side,
They all have fun. The war is forgotten.
When a Tommy scores a hat-trick, and the Germans agree,
When the game ends, they all shake hands,
All for the sake of war!

But Alas! Alack! The soldiers are called back!
By generals who are not pleased by the soldier's antics,
The bothered Brits send out a warning flare,
The gloomy Germans quickly renew their soldiers.
The Jerry's and the British soldiers surge forwards,
All for the sake of war!

Then line by line the soldiers go down,
Out of one hundred that go, only one returns.
That one had three friends, but they were all underage,
The soldiers' lives have permanently changed.
The bombing continues. So does the guns.
All for the sake of war!

Paradise Farr (11)
The John Roan School, London

STITCHES

I always wanted nine lives,
But maybe it's just me,
Figuring out that you broke my heart,
Wasn't the only thing left to see.

I believed every word you said,
But that was a stupid mistake,
You left me wandering the streets,
You did it once again.

You broke your promise to love me better,
So I see it was a dream,
Life hurts more than love,
Maybe life is just not for me.

That girl you left me for,
I hope she's happy,
'Cause all those memories of us,
Were left laying on the floor.

You took advantage of me,
All those times,
Now I need stitches,
To bring me back to life.

Morgen McCameron (11)
The John Roan School, London

HAMSTERS

For My Hamster Custard Cream

Hamsters,
Appreciative and kind,
Always there when you need someone to talk to.
Loving...

Hamsters,
Playful and energetic,
Always ready for a cuddle,
Cheeky...

Hamsters,
Investigative and mischievous,
Always trying to escape,
Smart...

Hamsters,
Loud and noisy,
Always ready for food,
Ravenous...

Hamsters,
Need a lot of work,
But worth it,
My best friend.

I love my hamster!

Ellie O'Mara (12)
The John Roan School, London

STARS THAT DON'T SHINE

These true feelings that tear me away from reality come from deep within,
A heart surrounded by steel can be healed by a love that runs in your veins,
Whether I am trapped in a trance of melancholy sadness,
Or full of shining light that lights up the darkest of tunnels,
You're always by my side,
More precious than the shimmering stars
That bring delight to the skies at their darkest hour.

I was separated from you by a tornado filled with feelings of hatred!
An eagle had killed the dove,
A door slammed in my face like a prison cell
Stopped my delicate heart from reaching you.
The stars no longer glittered like jewels in a princess's tiara,
Just balls of gas about to die,
In fact, they are already dead.
The world will eventually leave us without warning as nothing lasts forever,
Apart from my eternal soul that will face brutal battles to search for you,
A single tear fallen from a watery eye will never change the world,
But my heart and determination will guide me through my struggles,
I promised I would never fall again,
But it doesn't feel like falling,
Instead I am in deep water unable to breathe.
But I can still reach the top,
I can reach the shining lights that bring delight to the skies at night.

Amy Pogson Jones (12)
The John Roan School, London

ME, MYSELF AND I

I am a person who...
Likes to draw, read and watch all different kinds of things when I'm bored.
Hate waking up in the morning but love going to school.
I wish I could change...
The way I look
The way I feel around people.
And I have changed...
The way I behave
The way I am towards people
The way I am around people
But I like change because I can choose what I want to be changed.

Me, myself and I

Lucy-Anne Mitchell (12)
The John Roan School, London

POEM ON ENGLAND

England is beautiful from Aberdeen to Liverpool,
Padstow is pretty, Guernsey is good,
Jersey is joyful and Sussex just suits,
Royal Mail comes to pick up your post,
And BBC News gives you the groove.
Ireland to the west,
France to the south,
We are England and this is what it's all about.

William Bullen (12)
The John Roan School, London

THE CASTLE

Future ready, strong and steady,
Dungeons deep, towers tall,
Stone on stone, plank on plank,
Flags placed, seen all around,

Once,

Merry voices, stalls standing,
Fireplace burning, jaw crunching,
Cows grazing, clouds passing,
Soldiers sleeping, doors closing,

Once,

Fires blazing, rocks hurling,
Defences falling, walls crumbling,
Voices shouting, children crying,
Conquering without mercy is what was seen,

But now in ruins.

Adam Tolfree (11)
The John Roan School, London

FROGS ON FOGGY WATERS

Frogs hopping on clouds of mist
The water is steaming up into the air,
Clouds of grey,
Amongst the swamp water,
Are sometimes engulfed by the unusual waters.

Dylan Haynes (12)
The John Roan School, London

WASTELAND

Trees? Gone.
Blue sky? It's now a permanent smog.
Humanity is on the brink of extinction.
Who knows where this will take us... What's left?
Schools? Obliterated.
Oceans? A band of nothingness.
We've come together to defend what's left.
But we haven't got a single ounce of love.
This is a hopeless society.
Prayers? Silenced.
Smiles? Slipped away with sanity.
The world was prosperous, but now a downward slope.
We won't survive this if it's not stopped.
This is a wasteland.

Amelie Anne Denomme Watson (14)
The John Roan School, London

UNTITLED

As the sunlight bows down to a sky of shimmer,
All you can hear is a snake slither.
The moon around is a magnificent jewel in the sky,
So beautiful that if you even get close you'll surely die of awesomeness.

There is no sound but my own and as my stomach starts to groan,
It's time for a midnight snack!

Kiyan Mehre (12)
The John Roan School, London

WHAT IF?

A dilemma, that's what it was
A decision I had to make
Two paths going separate ways
Didn't know which one to take.

These two roads I carefully observed
Trying to find clues and signs
But they both seemed equally same
Two long deserted lines.

No hint to where they led
Only fog and white ahead
The skies slowly started crying
And life seemed to be dead.

Time was slowly running out
One path was wrong and the other right
So I took the one going left
Only because it had a brighter light

The path I chose led me to a destination
With a good life but too quiet and stiff
I don't regret the road I took
But I'll always ask myself 'What if?'

Erta Kupa (11)
The John Roan School, London

THE BOY WITH THE BIG BLUE EYES

The boy with big, blue eyes stands there watching me,
As I lay on the cold, hard ground and cry silently.
I wonder why he's not helping me,
But for some reason it doesn't surprise me.
The boy with big blue eyes comes closer.
And closer.
And closer.
Until he's right in front of me staring at me,
Closely,
He holds out a hand which I stare at hesitantly.
Until I take his hand and we stare into each other's eyes,
And in each other's eyes we see,
Sadness, happiness and love.
The sadness that feels my eyes every day.
The happiness that finally someone helps me.
Love as we both stare in each other's eyes.
Mine green, his blue.

Amber-Jade Hastings (11)
The John Roan School, London

MY FIRST DAY IN SCHOOL

There is a feeling in my stomach,
I don't know what it is,
It might be feelings of happiness,
Or feelings of tears,
I come out of the car,
Down the hill through the gate,
My mum holds my hand tightly,
Thinking, *Oh no, we're going to be late*,
I look around me,
Everyone smiling,
Some people crying,
Some people whining,
A thought tunnels its way in my head,
Everything's going to be all right.
I hold my head up high,
As brave as a knight,
I spot a boy,
A bit like me,
I walk up towards him,
He's grazed his knee,
I came across a teacher,
Looking very helpful,
I ask her for help,
She says, 'Aww, you're just not careful.'
The lady takes out a plaster,
Does her mends,
The boy gives me a thanking look,
Shhh, I think I might have found my first friend.

Muna Ahmedey (12)
The John Roan School, London

THE ODD DRAGON

Day after day and night after night,
Knowing that I will never get frostbite.
Red, after red, after red, after red,
Until the colours fade to the end.
Fire and screaming and lava and burning,
Ice and snow and laughter, just joking.
I wish that I could just join the crew,
But burning the world is the wrong thing to do.
Ice and fire do not go together,
That's probably why they hardly even bother.
Day after day thinking I want to change,
But when I look I think I am making a mistake.
Crumble, crack, crash and smash,
Now I just live in a place full of rubbish.
Screaming and crying and asking for help,
But I can't help as I'm something else.
Thinking and thinking as time goes by,
Watching them just fly by the sky.
The sun rises as the colour of my dreams,
Knowing I'm getting closer, in my 'dream'.
The shadow rises over the snow,
Thinking I'm special but really don't know.
Waking up in a pile snow,
And looking in front of me but just don't know.
Waking up in a pile of snow,
And looking in front of me but just don't know.
Bang, as a burnt piece of wood, lands on my wing,
As the ash takes over the snow like a king.
Red, orange and yellow consume the village,
I know now, red is the colour of death.
Burning the world is what they desire,
But I'll show them, never to play with fire.

Jai Cheung (11)
The John Roan School, London

THE END OF THE WORLD

Screams and shrieks pierce the air,
A hopeless place, a bleeding sky,
Open your eyes if you dare,
For the end of the world has come by.

A little girl, no more than ten,
Cries for her mum, cries for her dad.
For every person, a fallen tear,
The only sane in this world of mad.

Maybe you believe me, probably you don't.
But before you stop, carefully read my words.
For some day it might be you looking
At the remaining ashes of our once beautiful world.

When the time comes, a loud explosion,
Will forever deafen the humans of Earth.
And our sun, will turn against us,
While people curse their day of birth.

As the galaxy continues on,
Somewhere far, far away.
A light brighter than a burning star,
Will turn night into an endless day.

Chaos erupts, the planet awakens,
A living fire comes to destroy,
It's the burning flames of eternity
You know? With you the dead can toy.

There's no escape after that happens.
You can run but you can't hide.
Nowhere to go, nothing to do
The devils laughed and the angels cried.

Everything gone, nothing to mend,
The world has finally come to an end.

Eldona Kupa (13)
The John Roan School, London

MY SISTER, MY OTHER HALF

Drama here and there,
Not quite belonging anywhere.

Many tears are shed
And always seeing red.

Many people watch,
Many people laugh,
But eventually you'll stop and ask.

Friendships are made,
Friendships are broken
But ours will always be whole.

We make one,
But always apart
You are my bestie, my sister, my other half.

Esther Miller (14)
The John Roan School, London

I WISH

I wish that unicorns were true
I wish that all dreams were true
I once wished a lot of things were true
I wish for this...
The ocean to say hello
The ocean says happiness
The ocean is blue and always moving
Sometimes it fades and sometimes it stays.
This is the dream come true.

Shannon Dean (11)
The John Roan School, London

STRUGGLE

Online.
Offline.
Talking to strangers.
Having fun at midnight.
Walking in.
Walking out.
Same strangers as yesterday.
Same old crap as before.
Fake smiles.
Scarred arms.
The way of life.
Crying children.
Greyed graves.
Someone died there today.
Glazed eyes
Empty hearts
Her friends wake up empty and alone.
Diving into the blue.
You.
Them.
You all hurt her.
Sweet nothings.
Smoke scent.
That's all that's left of the loveliest girl.

Louise Collins (13)
The John Roan School, London

DREAMS

I sleep in the clouds,
Dream in the sky.
I'll keep dreaming,
As life passes me by
I think my dreams keep me sane
I dream of happiness
A life without pain.
The day seems good until you wake up.
The world seems welcoming until you enter it.
When the morning comes,
Nothing seems good
The moment my eyes open and until, they are shut.
Close your eyes and spread your wings
Make a wish and dream,
Good dreams
Don't ever say, you'll never tell.
'Cause life is too short and very frail.

Brenda Menyhart (13)
The John Roan School, London

FUTURE LIFE

I want to be in *future*
In 2020 with the age of
Twenty...
I will be a bird, which can fly up to really high
'Cause there is no time for me,
To stop and think twice.
If I die before, I finish wonderin'
I will reborn, making my new memory;
I will be in 2050
With nothing to worry me.
I can see the *future* through my eye
I can see a flying car in the bright blue sky,
Passing right in above me;
People are saying goodbye.
I will have lots of friends
That are made out of metal and steel,
They will be given a name called Robot.
Trust me it will be.
I will make my own house
From east to west,
Near the deep, dark blue ocean
Till I make it look best.
... This is the dream I share, and future of mine,
Pray to God and looking forward;
Until this tomorrow come,
And fly me away.

Sayaka Bhandari (14)
The John Roan School, London

MY HAPPINESS

I feel happy when I see light and colourful things,
Everything is better that way.
Fields of flowers and sunshine with birds that can sing,
I like that when it is day.

At dark I like it when everything is silent and nice,
It is one beautiful sight.
You cannot hear anything, not even mice,
I like that when it is night.

I smile when others are happy too,
It makes me think of joy and peace all day.
The last thing I worry about is being blue,
I hear others say:

Today I am thinking of positive thoughts,
Happiness is for me.
I want to meet people of all sorts,
That's happiness for you, you see.

The wind at the beach on a summer's morning
Walking on sand in the noon.
Laughing, smiling, giggling, talking,
Watching the shining moon.

That is what my day is like,
Going to places with loved ones that care
Even riding on my bike,
It makes me want to give you my poem to share.

Erin Jade Morgan (13)
The John Roan School, London

QUESTIONS OF A YOUNG TROUBLED TEEN

What is life?
What is the meaning?
One minute you're glad, next minute you're sad or mad.
You're never always happy, though good things happen there is always something that ruins your pleasure.
Why do we have to grow up?
Like Peter Pan I wish we could stay young forever.
Boring taxes, more rules and having a job.
I guess all I can say is live your young life to the fullest because you only live once
'YOLO'
Although being grown up is great being able to touch the trees that you could never reach before, never having a bedtime, being able to do what you want when you want and being able to eat the chocolates your mum said you couldn't have till tomorrow.
What is death?
Is there a Heaven or Hell?
Does it hurt?
So many questions but no answers who could I possibly ask?
All I can do is believe.
Just me, myself and I in this lonely world.
Even though I don't know what the future holds
All I can do is pray for another day.
Would I pass the Eleven plus?
What secondary school would I go?
The questions I asked myself last year planning out my life.
The truth is life never goes the way you expect it.
Will I ever find the secret of life?

Esther Joel (12)
The John Roan School, London

LIFE OF STEVE

A cuboid world
Pixellated alone
Fighting for survival
With your diamond sword.
Digging for emeralds, iron and gold
Mining and Crafting, you need to be bold.
Tunnelling and building your house and resources
Protecting your livestock and taming your horses.

A new day dawns, the sun is rising
A visitor! From a friendly land.
You Craft together and Mine the rocks
You build a boat down at your docks
You take a picnic, you go out fishing
In Minecraft it happens as easy as wishing!
An afternoon together creating the ultimate construction
The most amazing roller coaster - 'The Ride of Destruction!'

The sun is setting, It's time to leave,
A fantastic day with the other Steve.

Back to normal, jobs to be done
Wondering how long until the next day of fun.
Immersed in a cubular, parallel world
Angles and blocks, nothing is curled.

No family or wife
This is the life
Of Steve.

George Stepan (12)
The John Roan School, London

STARTING SCHOOL

Starting school is difficult,
Difficult class work,
Difficult homework,
Difficult relationships.

Everything is new,
New teachers,
New friends,
New school.

Everyone is different,
Different personalities,
Different appearances,
Different abilities.

You meet lots of people,
People who are boring,
People who are fun,
People who are enemies.
But you will get through it...

Rebecca Leigh (12)
The John Roan School, London

BEING A TEENAGER

Being a teenager involves,
More stress over homework,
Worrying that you don't fit in,
More pressure in school,
Worrying over the homework due in tomorrow,
More self-consciousness in public,
Worrying that you look weird,
More expectancy from people,
Worrying over harder responsibilities.

Being a teenager also involves,
More exciting changes in life,
You get more independence,
More interesting topics in school,
You find your own style,
More self decisions,
You find out more about the world,
More freedom in what you do,
You get older and wiser.

What else does being a teenager involve?

Ella Maria Josefiina Leppänen (13)
The John Roan School, London

WHERE IS LOVE?

I hope I can have a dinner or two,
With the person I love because I love you.
When I look into your eyes I see
The most beautiful stars glistening at me.
Our connection cannot be broken my love.

We were so happy and all our fear went away and disappeared.
But then a fight happened and you were gone.
As the doors shut I know that's the end,
Will I ever see you again my friend?
You cannot heal my broken heart
Because I knew it just can't be from the start.

You are the love of my life.
I will never let go.
We were like a dying rose hungry for thirst.
As all of mine and your dreams just burst.
We were like ashes from a fire.

Where is love?
Is it a flying dove?
I really don't know, but I wish I did.
I hope I will see you again
As our dreams just float away.

Agata Morgan (12)
The John Roan School, London

WHY MY HOMEWORK ISN'T HERE

About my homework Miss,
You can see it's not here.
Well believe me Miss,
I did see it here.
I was doing my homework,
When I found myself
Flying really high,
In the big blue sky.
I was kidnapped by a Russian man,
Sat down by a Scottish fan.
I was magicked into a log,
Then I was turned into white fog.
I was - yes miss?
'Detention for lying about all of this'
'I tell you, this story was quite real,
For if it was fake I'd be a weasel.'

Joe Tuffee (11)
The John Roan School, London

WAR, WAR, WAR...

War, war, death and gore, no more evil anymore,
These trenches smell like hell.
I can't wait until the victory bell.

War, war, death and gore, no more evil anymore,
As I stand on the front line,
I watch my fellow soldiers die,
One at a time.

War, war, death and gore, no more evil anymore,
As I lie on my deathbed my head spinning round and round.
I think about my beloved wife and my wonderful life.

Olivia Melvin
The John Roan School, London

A POEM TO THE NUMBER 30

30 boys and girls, all sitting in a tree
30 crying babies, all spitting out their tea

30 broken teenage hearts needing to be fixed
30 Christmas puddings all needing to be mixed.

30 days in a month, unless there's 31
30 ice cubes on my foot make me feel quite numb

You'll find that 30 minutes will make half an hour
Which, coincidentally, is the time my sister takes to shower.

The standard school ruler is 30cm long
A polygon with 30 sides is called triacontagon.

30 science teachers who try and make me think
30 is the atomic number of shiny metal zinc.

When I reach the age of 30, I'll feel kind of old
And presumably my school books will have grown a lot of mould.

Swimming with my father, he'll do 30 lengths
My best so far is 21, we've all got different strengths.

We're halfway through my poem, which is 30 lines long
I think you'll find the rhymes are getting pretty strong.

I searched around the Internet for things that come in 30s
But quickly found my brain was getting kind of hurty.

My primary school was finished when the clock struck three thirty
But now I work all day and night with no mercy.

My favourite team is Arsenal the goalie's name is Cech
But he is number 33, not 30, oh heck!

I asked my mum to tell me what happened 30 years ago
She said Top Gun, big hair, shoulder pads - yo!

We're nearing 30 lines my friends, I bet you feel relieved
Next up is the end, if that's something you can believe.

It's funny when you ask someone what 30 means to them
You'll find the list they give will make an award winning poem.

Alfred Pryke (11)
The John Roan School, London

WAR AND LOSS

As the war keeps going on,
Explosions make waves and whispers,
I run towards the evacuating ships,
Germans firing like lions roaring.
Keep silent to not to be blown up.

More and more buildings have been burning,
Where is my only brother who lies and slay,
I need to hide before I get caught,
By the time I get out here it will be swarmed with an army,
I'll have to wait it will be freezing,
As quick as a flash I run to the main hall,
As fast as a cheetah.
Boom! I stood still on my knees,
Slowly fell, my hands are covered with blood,
Lay there as the guns went quiet,
As I said my last words.

Jamie Majomi (11)
The John Roan School, London

I WISH

I wish I could climb the highest mountain,
I wish I had a mate to watch over me.
I wish I had no worries about the outside world.
I wish I knew how to live my own way.
I wish I could live with no danger around every corner.
I wish there was only love and happy times.
I wish I could leave all this sadness and anger.
I wish there was world peace and happiness.
I wish we could only be happy.
I wish we could all get along.
How I wish there was freedom in our world!

Sophie May Prizeman (11)
The John Roan School, London

ANIMAL POEM

Animals are cool,
Animals rule,
Yeah!
Down with plants!
Cute or ugly
Furry or smooth
Animals around us
So respect them
Like I respect you,
Animals are cool,
Animals rule,
Yeah!
Down with plants!
They give you company
It's not much to ask
So when you achieve something,
Pull out a flask!
Yeah!
Animals are cool,
Animals rule,
Yeah!
Down with plants!
Cats are cute and cuddly,
They all are unique
They are awesome!
Animals are cool,
Animals rule
Yeah! Yeah!

Amber Louise Pledge (11)
The John Roan School, London

THE WIND

As the wind awakes,
The whole world quakes.

The wind rumbles,
And tumbles and tumbles.

As the wind glares,
It blows all your hair.

The wind howls and howls,
And scares the owls.

As the wind strikes,
It rustles at all the bikes.

The wind snores and
Smashes the doors.

As the wind whispers
And whispers and whispers some more.

The wind roars
Not to be seen any more.

Amy Carolan (12)
The Sacred Heart Language College, Harrow

DARKNESS

I am a person of survival
But growing that was not really my title
Stuck in the dark, too scared to show up.
But I've grown up better than before
I'm invincible and perfect in my own way.
You can't hurt me and that's the truth at the end of the day.

Sekura Queensborough (13)
The Sacred Heart Language College, Harrow

NIGHTMARES

The clock strikes midnight
Shadows come out in the moonlight
Our worst dreams come alive
Into our imaginations they dive.

They kill our wildest dreams
Make us sing silent screams
They creep into our minds
Now I see all the danger signs.

They will not just go
They will turn into your foe
They are light and dark
As unfriendly as a shark.

They invade our happiest memories
And create terrific tragedies
They stab our imaginations
And destroy our creations.

What was once a sweet pony
Was left lonely
And transformed into a simple, sorrowful and sedentary rock
By the death-bringing eyes of one of Medusa's serpents right in front of the clock.

The story makes me fear
Sounds of screams I can hear
We wake up in the moonlight
Mum says, 'Keep calm everything is all right'
We sleep again
They will come back but I don't know when.

Carolina Isabel Vieira Fernandes (12)
The Sacred Heart Language College, Harrow

THE REALITY WORLD

The phones, the laptops and televisions,
Don't improve people's visions.
However, the people into the screens stare,
When they have some time spare.

The magical fantasy world it is indeed,
However, there is a lot of people in need.
People with worries,
And with awful sad stories.

After all, the Earth is not such a magical place,
But it is the best in the whole outer space!
This is the reality world!

Alicja Majewska (12)
The Sacred Heart Language College, Harrow

THE BEACH

I stood still on the soft golden sand
And ran, the fresh water through my hand
What a beautiful place I could see
What a beautiful place to be.

I looked out at the scene
And how lucky I had been
The birds tweeted on a sweet song
I forgot about all the wrong.

All the death, sin and pain
What a shame
What a wonderful place
I won't be leaving in a haste.

Maggie Reddington (12)
The Sacred Heart Language College, Harrow

OMG SOCIAL MED

Why is everyone on Twitter,
Being a lemon? So bitter!
From all the conversations that I'm finding there,
It seems that society simply doesn't care.

Your mailing lists are a right joke.
On the file, there's always a hoax.
When I am doing my work, it always buts in
Now I keep on pressing that fake cancel button.

Don't get me started on Facebook.
All those selfies that that girl took.
With family or friends, it never seems to end.
All with the duck face, an irreversible trend.

Oh and then there's that Tumblr,
The problem? There's a number.
The whole site is a complete waste of time
If there was a value, it'll be less than a dime.

What a waste of time, Instagram
The whole stupid site is a sham
Puppies in cups and cats wearing bread aren't cute!
If I was much older, I would put a lawsuit.

I don't know if it is just me,
But I feel to beg on my knee,
Just delete all those blooming apps before I scream
'Delete the whole social media scene!'

Vanessa Litha Banda (12)
The Sacred Heart Language College, Harrow

THE SUMMER

The sun so bright,
The burning of the light.
The blue ocean sways,
On the scorching shore he lays.
The melting of ice cream,
The children's faces with gleam.
And as the birds sing a peaceful hymn,
And on hot days the children swim.
Oh the joy of flying high up in the sky,
It is almost impossible to say goodbye.

Jessica Maquiece Faty Mbala (12)
The Sacred Heart Language College, Harrow

ME

They found it there on the cold, hard floor.
Twisted shape propped against the door.
If it wasn't he and it wasn't she
Who slapped the thigh and smashed the knee.
Pulled the lips into a thin, tight line.
Pushed out the breath into a whine.
Lifted the brows as if to ask.
Held the gaze as if a mask.
Bullet holes from woes departed
The victim has clearly been outsmarted
I don't know who this thing could be.
If it wasn't he, could it be me?

Lauren John-Charles (13)
The Sacred Heart Language College, Harrow

GRANDAD'S SPARE ROOM

It was only the spare room
The nobody there room
The presence in the air room
The unbearable spare room.

It wasn't the guest room
The designed to impress room
The four poster best room
The return to the nest room.

It wasn't the main room
The humble and plain room
The up front and vain room
The plumped up and plaid room.

It wasn't the head room
The blue or red room
The creep on your feet room
The baby's asleep room.

It wasn't the bright room
The light on all night room
The very uptight room
The hide out of sight room.

Empty, lonely, cold and dark
Silent, peaceful, bare and stark

It was only the spare room
The nobody there room
The presence in the air room
The unbearable spare room.

Lois O'Flaherty (12)
The Sacred Heart Language College, Harrow

BAD BOTTLED UP EMOTIONS

Pitch-black without a sound
The kiss it gives winds me round
A strong wound I receive as I pound into the ground
Stomp! Stomp! Stomp! I hear it coming
Like the endless catacomb of a large drum drumming
The eyes are blood-red with a menacing glow as anonymous size seems to grow
Under the eyes it is baggy like sacks
Not forgetting the leaf-green prickles all over its back
Running as fast as a cheetah, no spots
Crying and screaming as if a lonely baby in a cot
Imagine how you'd feel to never laugh, never cry
That's how I felt when I was running. But now you'll ask me, why?
This monstrosity haunting my thoughts with every move
Making my blood dance is something else I can prove
You've asked let me answer: I really don't know
Although that it's spring I feel cold as ice and snow
Whatever you may think it's approaching at a high speed
This causes me to panic much more than I need
What is this thing that makes me scream at the mention of its name?
I bet it thinks that I'm just playing a game
The monster that follows me is impossible to tame
Oh when I am free how I will exclaim
The pain of the secret I've kept so close
I feel a thorn in the back as if from a rose
Silently I fall like a feather
A large shadow above me. It wasn't the weather
It reached for me with its sharp clawed finger
I tried to run but it made me linger
The monster coming. Where am I? Only beside
That's what all my emotions feel like when they're bottled up inside.

Nicole Moyo (13)
The Sacred Heart Language College, Harrow

AWAKENING NATURE

How peaceful the world became
As nature awakened again
Hearing waterfalls drifting down the lake
But the sight made my breath take.

Can you hear the birds calling?
Just hearing them say good morning,
Makes my heart smile,
Knowing it will be worthwhile.

Beyond the waves, beyond the wind,
Beyond the world we live in,
Away from the bright lights and noisy cars,
Beneath the sky of glistening stars,

Just look at nature's way,
On a midsummer's day,
The sun shone bright like a diamond,
As the excitement within me tightened,

How peaceful the world became
As nature awakened again
Take a moment to inhale,
And listen to Nature as she tells her tale.

Essence Walters-Williams (12)
The Sacred Heart Language College, Harrow

DRIP-DROP

Drip-drop
On the rainy solemn day,
On the fourth of May,
Lived an old woman called Shay.

Drip-drop
She went down the stairs,
Crossed a hall full of chairs,
And went to a bathroom decorated in bears.

Drip-drop
She turns on the lights,
And saw her greatest of frights,
Her cat hung from great heights.

Drip-drop
Went his blood,
On the ground like a puddle of mud.

Drip-drop
She turned around,
And her heart began to pound,
When the monster had her found,
As her scream became an echoing sound.

Patrycja Lukasiewicz (14)
The Sacred Heart Language College, Harrow

THE CAVE OF LONELINESS

The cave of loneliness,
With rocks like shells.
A single stick burns,
It burns for no one.

The cave entrance stays open,
It waits for no one.
The whistling wind blows on the fire,
Crack, crackle, crack.

The rustling leaves,
Blow through the cave,
Whistling, rustling and whirling around,
They blow for no one.

Not a single person walks in sight,
The cliff steps wait for the person that will never come.

Isabella Dalpat (11)
The Sacred Heart Language College, Harrow

A DREAM

What a dream, is it small or big?

I've always had a dream,
That unicorns are eating ice cream.

I've always had a dream,
That I could walk on a stream.

I've always had a dream,
That I was on the cheerleading team.

I've always had a dream,
That I would be standing on a gymnastics beam.

I've always had a dream,
What would be yours?

Danielle Arday (12)
The Sacred Heart Language College, Harrow

THE ONE I LOST

It was an ordinary day
And I was sitting on a bay
Wondering if we'll be okay
And if we'll ever be the same.

It was as sudden as a hurricane
Like unexpected rain
I lost him and he lost me
A friend I can't replace.

And now I'm sitting here alone
Feeling like your foe
Drowning in my thoughts at home
I'm crying on my own
My tears filling up my soul.

Nikola Anna Maciejowska (13)
The Sacred Heart Language College, Harrow

BABIES

Lots of babies like to sleep
But when you're in the car don't ever press the beep
Sometimes all they do is cry
Remember to keep them occupied.

They go toilet in their nappies that's why we call them leakers
They want everybody that's why we call them attention seekers
During their younger years they don't get blamed
But for the rest they get named and shamed.

Don't forget babies are soft and kind
If you tried to be like them I'm sure they won't mind
Their favourite game is copy cat
And when they feel like burping, give them a big pat!

Kendi Hunter-Lander (11)
The Sacred Heart Language College, Harrow

IN THE GARDEN OF ENCHANTMENT

In the garden of enchantment
The fairies dance
And in the ruins
The memories linger
Whilst the wind whispers in your ear
It fills your soul with magic.

In the garden of enchantment
The pixies skip
And the ghosts so pale
Haunt this place of wonder
It captivates your curious eyes
And makes you think, *What has happened here?*

In the garden of enchantment
The trolls grunt
And the supernatural silhouettes
Slip through the shadows
But only at midnight you can see this mystery
So goodbye from all the magic
In the garden of enchantment.

Rebecca Painter (11)
The Sacred Heart Language College, Harrow

SCHOOL IS A BORE

Oh Mummy I'm too sick to go to school
If you send me you would be a fool.
All that work on fractions give me a shiver,
In PE we do forty laps which hurt my liver.
Adjectives are such a bother,
Please don't send me oh mother.
Yesterday we dissected a heart,
Maths will make me constantly fart.
The Romans are so old,
And the heating is broken so it's really cold.
School makes me rage,
It is like a giant cage.
I think a girl has given me her chickenpox,
My eardrums will blow if I hear the tick of the clock.
School is a bore,
And I know learning is a chore.
But Mummy I'm not going, okay?
Oh yeah, it's Saturday.

Holly Kellett Quince (11)
The Sacred Heart Language College, Harrow

DREAMS

As silent as a butterfly wing,
Comes at dusk, goes at dawn,
In our heads, they will sing,
At night, they will be worn.

Some come fast or slow,
Some come hot or cold,
They will always just go,
They are made of gold,

They are like paradise,
They go too soon,
Their beauty is like sunrise,
As pure as the full moon,

As they stick like glue,
They work in teams,
As they are new,
These are called dreams.

Natalie Emmens (13)
The Sacred Heart Language College, Harrow

THE LIFELESS BODY

My enemy I saw,
Lying upon the shore,
Lifeless in every way,
Then the day it slipped away.

As I came near,
My heart racing with fear,
For he sprang up,
Was this the end of my luck?

I knew what I had to do, it was hard all the same
But this was not a game
I dug in the knife I held in my hand,
The blood flowed along the sand.

It was over now,
And only I knew how,
My foe had died,
That's what I sighed.

Grace Hovey (12)
The Sacred Heart Language College, Harrow

THE SEA AND OCEAN

Every morning you wake up to the gleaming sea,
It fills you with joy and glee,
The gentle waves across your face,
The sea couldn't be a better place,
You have a barrier so you can breathe,
How good is that, would you believe?
Dolphins, Nemos, any type of fish,
It almost seems just like a myth,
A paradise in the ocean, full of memories,
Tastes like the sweet berries of life,
But yet still as sharp as a knife,
There is a dark side to the sea,
One that is not so happy,
Darkness lurks beneath the ocean,
Where there is no motion,
You never know when it might happen,
However you will hear a sound,
From across the mound,
Return to the surface,
But remember the sea,
The sea that fills you with joy and glee.

Mayá Wilson (11)
The Sacred Heart Language College, Harrow

THE SEASIDE

Playing on the silky sand what fun it could be,
The bright sun gleaming on us,
Dancing along in glee.

As the lotion is applied there is such a big fuss,
Three little children diving into the sea,
The other two playing football on the beach.

All the adults gathered around, to order some tea.
The jet skis were making some noise,
In the clear blue sea.

The calm waves splashed,
As the little children clashed.
Though as it started to rain everyone fled.

But the little children cried in dread,
Alas, they fled from the resort,
So as they arrived at the port.

Mela Sarah Musie (11)
The Sacred Heart Language College, Harrow

THE BEACH

Waves bash against sand
As if they are enemies
The waves retreat and

Crash

The waves strike again
Like a perpetual loop
Without any end

Sea stretches its arms
Engulfs me in its embrace
It's one of its charms.

The sun hits my eye
Packs a big powerful punch
Never is it shy.

The bay just stands still
It's reliable and safe
Are the waves?

Eliana Padalino (13)
The Sacred Heart Language College, Harrow

DEPRESSION

I don't want to die,
All alone I have to be,
I'm not saying bye,
No one is even with me.

The walls are closing in,
The air is glazed with suspense,
The sweat is dripping off my chin,
Oh why is this so tense?

Peering through the slippery bars,
It's breaking my heart,
I shouldn't have to part,
With my darling sweetheart!

My mind is confused,
My body is tormented,
My eyes are closing,
My hands are shrivelling.

Will I ever mend?
No,
For this is the end...

Grace Aleksandra McHugh (12)
The Sacred Heart Language College, Harrow

AFRICA

The morning breeze,
The golden sunshine,
Go find your own,
It's all mine.

Exotic, wild creatures,
Can't wait to see,
Africa,
That will reveal to me.

Lions, zebras,
And many more,
Elephant, cheetahs,
And things that soar.

Traditional dancers,
Not one... two... three,
But swishing and swaying,
Harder than the sea.

Hear the owls hooting away,
What I see is the moonlight,
In Africa a sight that can't wait,
But now I've got to say goodnight.

Rachel Irabor (12)
The Sacred Heart Language College, Harrow

MIRROR IMAGE

I am the mirror,
I see all,
All of your imperfections,
The things that disgust and appal

Your face covered in pimples,
Like a mountainous plain,
With spots the size of Mars,
You try to hide them in vain.

Your body so fat,
That it spills out the sides,
The dresses that look so good on others,
Never perfectly fit your size.

You're never truly beautiful,
Your hair is like a mop,
It hangs limply down,
But frizzes on top.

And don't get me started on fashion,
You never follow the trends,
You just stand there like a scarecrow,
Not as pretty as any of your friends.

But I am just a mirror,
My job is to reflect,
It's you that projects these insecurities,
There's no such thing as perfect.

Eleanor Horne (13)
The Sacred Heart Language College, Harrow

THE GREEN EYE

My eyes are the colour blue,
But then they change when I see you,
I try to stay strong, I really try,
But I fail because of the green eye.

You fill me full of desire,
Making my envy even higher,
I try to keep it in, I really try,
But I still fail because of the green eye.

You make my insecurities fill,
Making your happiness tempting to kill,
I somehow make both you and me cry,
All because of the green eye.

Your perfection just makes me mad,
But your suffering doesn't make me glad,
I struggle to stay strong, I just can't try,
It is just this loathed green eye.

I couldn't take it anymore,
It caused my face to hit the floor,
My anger had just got too high,
And that was the end of my green eye.

Lorianne Swift (12)
The Sacred Heart Language College, Harrow

SLEEPING BEAUTY

Do you know what it's like to sleep all year?
Until you wake up facing your true dear,
I lay in bed like a swan sitting on eggs,
My love riding on a horse steady with his legs.

While I sleep I feel horror all around,
Not knowing if I will ever touch the ground,
Thinking of my prince dying in the thorns,
And my worst nightmare... eating prawns.

If I wake up I will be a flower,
Tall and proud even in a tower,
I will have a dress and wear lipstick strawberry red,
And forget that my city was even dead!

The only thing I do remember before I fell asleep,
Was I pricked my finger and slept deep,
I remember my father, annoyed with every game I won,
But still we had so much fun.

But now I know it's all over,
I am in the park finding a four leaf clover,
Sitting down with my prince holding my hand,
So tired, I can't even stand!

Olivia Cole Keller (11)
The Sacred Heart Language College, Harrow

WITHOUT MY PHONE

Being without my phone,
Makes me feel alone.
For the past I've had Internet friends,
But now my life slowly bends.
Realising things without my phone,
Tells me things I've never known.
I used to think my phone was everything,
But now I know that it's just for texting.

For the weeks I have discerned my sister is injured
For I've been chatting as my battery life flickered.
Sooner and sooner I see the growing of gadgets,
The thought of it is like we are on different planets.

Sometimes they could be handy,
Or can be bad like a shot of brandy.
It can be there for the bad things,
Such as accidents on swings.
You can call people for emergencies,
Such as a scary tragedy.

But, being without my phone,
Doesn't make me alone
I don't need Internet friends
Now my life slowly extends.
Realising many things without it,
Told me things I got to know.
But I still need my phone.

Kanisha Kumaran (12)
The Sacred Heart Language College, Harrow

MY LITTLE MITTENS

Big fluffy paws,
Sticks its tongue out when it yawns,
And running in and out of halls.
Oh I love my kitten,
Her name is Mittens.

Always taking a nap
Lies on my lap,
And loves her mat.
Oh I love my cat,
Used to be a kitten,
And her name is Mittens.

Never comes out to play,
Uses her litter tray,
And hates the rain's gentle spray.
Oh how I still love my cat,
Used to lie on my lap,
Used to be a kitten,
And her name is Mittens.

Always sleepy,
But never weepy,
And always loves me.
Oh how I will always love my cat,
She lies on my lap,
Adores her mat,
Used to be a kitten,
And her name is Mittens.

Although you may look boring,
You'll never leave me snoring,
You are always my little kitten,
And I call you my little Mittens.

Cara McNally (11)
The Sacred Heart Language College, Harrow

TRAPPED

Walking home and I can see
Birds flitting peacefully.
The sky is filled with pools of blue
And grass sparkles with morning dew.
But catch a glinting eye like steel
The perfection suddenly feels unreal.
Taken away from beautiful blue
Clouds of grey come into a view.
Looming figures steal your mind.
Perfect and peaceful is left behind.
Your legs start running faster than time
But a voice creeps in saying 'You're mine.'
Your gaze wanders to a shady hill
Suddenly your heart stops still.
Lightning strikes inside your head
Midnight chimes, you join the dead.

Elizabeth Adeyemi (12)
The Sacred Heart Language College, Harrow

WAR

The sky once blue
Now covered black,
The ocean once vast and wide,
Seems now so small,
Whilst metal sharks roam above,
And the wolves of the deep come out to hunt.

The mountains and land,
Once vast and plentiful,
Now covered in ash and blood,
While metal demon clash and,
Metal eagles collide with metal hawks,
In the skies above,
Enduring a dance of Death.

Tatianna-Rose Marie Weymouth-Shanks (12)
The Sacred Heart Language College, Harrow

THE FUTURE TECHNOLOGY

The technology will be developed on its own,
You don't need to do anything for yourself
The future is uncertain, that you can't see
Wait for it till tomorrow.
For the day it's going to be,
For you to see the glee.
You flee in the presence of the technology,
As you are floating on the clouds.
With technology, I am going walkabouts.
God invented the humans, and humans invented the technology.
But when the technology discontinues, the world falls apart,
And the people have to work on their own,
Without any invention all by themselves sitting in their homes.
What do you do now?

Jenith Andrea Soundararajan (12)
The Sacred Heart Language College, Harrow

WHY IS IT SO HARD?

Why is it so hard?
We stood there in the dark
Hand in hand to make a mark
We're supposed to be a family
Why is it so hard for you to see?

My life is so hard now you are here
My life was so soft
My life was so calm
Why do you have to make it so difficult?

You were my first
Your were my last
You were my life
Why can't you see that?

Kaira George (13)
The Sacred Heart Language College, Harrow

WHERE THE SIDEWALK ENDS

There is a place where the sidewalk ends
And before the streets begins,
And there the grass grows soft and white,
And there the sun burns crimson bright,
And there the moon-bird rests from his flight
To cool peppermint wind.

Let us leave this place where the smoke blows back
And the dark street winds and bends.
Past and pits where asphalt flowers grow
We shall walk with a walk that is measured and slow,
And watch where the chalk-white arrows go
To the place where sidewalks ends.

Yes, we'll walk with a walk that is measured and slow,
And we'll go where chalk-white arrows go,
For the children, they mark,
And the children,
They know
The place where sidewalks end.

Georgine Albaque (13)
The Sacred Heart Language College, Harrow

COMA

I lay motionless and dispirited like a skeleton on a slick blue hospital sheet.
Voices, chatter, tears
Sorrowful mourns and prayers of hopeful people who meet.
Gathering around to share their fears.

Was I so foolish as to risk my own life?
I am here for my own doing.
I just had to start the strife.
Mortified, I am, for it was my own childish choosing.

Eyes shut tight pale white face shows no expression.
Another misty day, another fragile jail.
I cry aloud but all in session.
But would I make it? Would I fail?

Because I could not stop for death,
But, it won't prevail to find me.
Life awaits just around the corner, just one more breath.
If only he would kindly stop for me.

Muffled sounds but my heart is fighting strong.
A slight chance of death, but I could be wrong.
My time could be up any moment so, so long.
But I could make it I can ma-

Jessica Odukwu (13)
The Sacred Heart Language College, Harrow

FAKE SMILES

You may think she's the happiest person around,
Outside she may be active and loud.
Besides the pretence there's a side to her nobody knows,
Her mind constantly soaked in great woes.

She may continuously say that she's okay,
Owns a catalogue of lies to get her own way.
Prefers to be in the presence of seclusion,
Pervades her mind with thoughts of delusion.

A disguise that has maintained the secrecy of its identity,
Is worn whilst she searches for serenity.
Each night she lay with the same vision,
That very soon she may fade into oblivion.

Her thoughts had thoroughly been hindered,
With the realisation her life had been injured.
However fake smiles take daily control over her face,
To veil her burdening case.

Nadia Ampofo (13)
The Sacred Heart Language College, Harrow

THE DOG

The dog woofs as the postman arrives,
Running to his owner he cries,
I want food now or I will cry.

When he hears his owner mix his food,
He runs into the kitchen room
Eating up his rice and chicken.

What a lovely dinner,
Like a lightning bolt he eats,
Eating down his chicken chunks.

Jasmine Wadhwani (12)
The Sacred Heart Language College, Harrow

THE CITY THAT WILL NEVER STOP

In the derelict city of uncertainty,
Street lights flicker like the stutter of a voice,
Buildings neglected like a heart being torn in two.
The whisper of the wind is only to be found.

Streets, perilous, crammed full of unrest,
As the sky, ghostly, lifeless.
Don't dare venture into the blood-curdling city.

The rumble of a car like a hungry stomach is not to be caught,
Nor the ramble of chatter never grim.
Yet in the deep dingy shadows,
Lurk the ghost that once dastardly dwelled,
Who glares eyes of wrath
On those who enter.

This was the city,
This is the city,
This will be the city,
That never slept.

Eilis Bourke (12)
The Sacred Heart Language College, Harrow

THE WIND

The wind is a calm mother
Delicate and soft.
I open my window and the warm ripples
Gently kiss my face.
She sings me a lullaby with her soothing voice.

Suddenly she changes her tone,
Full of rage.
She becomes aggressive and violent.
She shatters my window,
With a howling screech.
In the dark of night.

Shanai Ranasinghe (12)
The Sacred Heart Language College, Harrow

FROZEN

Frozen, solid,
How long had I slept for?
Ice all around,
Not a glimpse of humanity,
Icicles hanging from every object,
But it wasn't winter!

There was nothing left,
The ice burnt down the city,
The icicles were soldiers,
Lined up in battle formation
The icy floor a no-man's-land,
This was once London.

The Shard, gone,
Big Ben, gone,
Tower Bridge, gone,
London, gone
Everything, gone
I was the only person left.

Zoe Grace McCormack (12)
The Sacred Heart Language College, Harrow

SILENCE

Silence.
It filled the air and encaged the room,
Not a sound could be heard, not a crash, not a boom,
But in the boy's mind was a violent war,
Of shouts and screams, his confidence it tore,
Bullets of self-hatred piercing the boy,
Depression straggling him and suffocating his joy,
The cannon of harmful words firing at will,
Completing his mission that was to find happiness and kill,
A waterfall of quiet tears streaming down his face,
Drowning any hope of his euphoria murder case,
Giving up on finding a reason to smile,
A permanent frown showing he is no longer in denial,
Letting his demon called Misery control,
No longer keeping up his cheerful child acting role,
All his gleeful memories sucked into a black pit,
Of emptiness and loneliness that always seemed to hit,
His mind being abused by the negativity,
His heart being ripped by painful activity,
Although he feels he no longer can hide,
From the sinister monster that's eating him inside,
The boy has a padlocked mouth, shutting down any chance,
Of revealing his bottled-up emotions in any circumstance,
So in the room he cowers, hoping the monsters will go away,
Not making a single sound and letting them say what they say,
But one day he hopes that he will hear that wonderful sound,
Showing him his life ruining demons are no longer around,
Silence.

Milly Cooney (13)
The Sacred Heart Language College, Harrow

A MERMAID'S DAY

Splash, splash, splash,
Mermaids playing in the water,
Brushing their hair with coral leaves
Going to sleep on soft coral weeds,
Waking up to the sound of sweet singing dolphins,
Going to collect more seaweed,
Above water they lay on a rock,
And sing so peacefully and beautifully
Some of them out of the water,
Onto the soft glowing sand,
It is time for them to go back to the salty sea and go to sleep on the coral weed.

Lauren Austin-Glass (11)
The Sacred Heart Language College, Harrow

THE YEAR 3016

The year 3016,
Where the world comes to an end.
Tall falling buildings and bridges bend.
Alien invasion, humanity extinct,
Whose fault is it, maybe a clinch.

No more tech, no more luxuries
Who knows how long this will go on for,
Maybe centuries.
Burning cars, crispy trees
One survivor down on their knees.

Falling debris, smoking leaves
The stinky corpses smell like cheese
My time is near, time is free
This is year 3016.

Kayla Ivana Quarshie (12)
The Sacred Heart Language College, Harrow

IS THAT YOU...?

Goodnight my darling, goodnight,
I hope the naughty bed bugs don't bite.
We talk, laugh and sleep,
Don't go beep, beep, beep.

My parents are gone,
I'm still awake.
Oh no for goodness sake,
It's scary now and scary then.
Humming coming from the wardrobe,
My mum's not home, what should I do...?

Kacey June McDonald (11)
The Sacred Heart Language College, Harrow

MEMORIES OF MY MOTHER

Blood creeping in my dreams,
I have a fear of my mother's screams,
Her delicate touch, her loving smile,
Her long blonde hair, her amazing style.

The sound of her soft voice, so sweet,
This was what made my life complete,
The house is quiet and still,
I pass her room, I feel a chill.

My dad, a violent wrecking ball,
Smashes the glass against the wall,
His verbal attacks, I cannot bear,
His happy smiles are now so rare.

For I would give it all,
Just to hear her say,
It's going to be okay.

Jessica McIntyre (12)
The Sacred Heart Language College, Harrow

HOW HAS TECHNOLOGY CHANGED THE WORLD?

How has technology changed the world!
Or has it changed at all?
Our minds could be mashed or even smashed
Or possibly quite curled.

How has technology changed the world?
Will it change in the future?
Microwaves cook our food if we are not in the mood.
And phones do everything for us.

How has technology changed the world?
Social has become media
Our world has become Internet, our lives have been set.
We are officially the laziest on Earth.

How has technology changed the world?
TV is now a main essential
Apple is the place to go, to tell you everything from head to toe.
It is quite sad, that pen and paper no longer exists.

How has technology changed the world?
Is it for the better or for worse?
This is modern day, where we have to pay
Technology is here to stay.

Cassie Olympia Fernandes (11)
The Sacred Heart Language College, Harrow

HE LEFT ME

He left me. Broken. Today
Trailing his scuffed shoes on the pathway
A hole formed in my heart and mind
Growing huge, it didn't subside.

My sadness dissolved, but anger came
Without my soulmate, it wasn't the same
My body began to shake.
Knuckles bleeding, I punched the mirror making it break.

I couldn't hold it back any more
My anger had burst out, making my body feel sore
My world had come to a sudden end
All I needed was a kind friend.

Howling softly, my heart was torn in two
I wish I was lucky enough, to be like you
I sat on a broken chair, but only a framed photograph of me and him was all I could see
The back of grey walls, is the only life for me.

Erin Pitts (12)
The Sacred Heart Language College, Harrow

STAGE FRIGHT

I trembled with fear written on my face,
My heart pounded at an amazing pace.

Chaos filled the frantic atmosphere,
It was all a blur and very unclear

We stood in silence, waiting patiently,
Restlessly waiting while sat silently

The terror kept my heart pumping,
With my adrenaline rapidly flowing

I stepped out into the eerie darkness,
Frantically running into gloomy vastness

The stage was empty and all was calm,
I could feel the sweat dripping down my palm

Without a warning the music commenced,
I could feel the tension, this was going to be immense

My mind was engaged as I pranced about,
My heart beat in counts of eights, I had no doubt.

The lights got dim until there was complete darkness,
A loud cheer came from the pitch-black emptiness

There isn't much left to say,
Except it was silly to be scared that day.

Olivia Inniss (12)
The Sacred Heart Language College, Harrow

THE ROBOT

The robot walks on hard, cold ground,
Screeching with a metal sound,
He lasers down the passers-by,
As quickly as swatting a pesky fly.

He stalks through the dusty streets,
And humans look down at their feet,
As they see the fearsome Lord,
Whose lasers strike you like a sword.

They cower in their dirty holes,
As the monstrous machine lulls,
His latest victim to their doom,
And lasers them with a mighty zoom!

He clears his world of dirt and filth
Silently he madly kills,
Everyone who's in his way,
He might even get to you one day.

Frances Parkinson (11)
The Sacred Heart Language College, Harrow

JUDGING OTHERS

Judging others is a serious crime,
It causes pain and shame.
Whoever judges is truly awful and lame.

Judging others is a sin against God.
Once you start, you don't stop at all,
So change for the better or else you'll fall.

People who are gay, lesbian, bisexual or straight,
Are still all humans that God has made,
So why judge and try and make their feelings fade.

So why judge at all if it is against God's rules.
Are you trying to make them feel bad?
Or are you just doing it because you are sad?

Think, don't judge!

T'yana Nee-Chambers (12)
The Sacred Heart Language College, Harrow

WORDS

They're not human, but they hurt like one.
They're not human, but they spread around.
They're not human, but they can hold you down.

They're not a friend; they're like a punch in the stomach.
They're not a friend, but they're always there.
They're not a friend, but you can feel their stare.

They're hurtful, and can cause you pain.
They're hurtful; your tears fall like rain.
They're hurtful, again, and again, and again.

Words are not big, but they're not small.
They are the most hurtful things of all.

Isabel Earls
The Sacred Heart Language College, Harrow

HOMELESS

In a dark, damp street,
With my cold feet,
Who should I tell,
I don't yell,
I have no food to eat
Just a box and some newspaper for heat

'Can I have some money?' I say,
'I just need a place to lay,'
What should I go to,
Can I cope?
Or should I just pray for hope?

You don't need to care,
It's just not fair,
I can't have any fun,
I don't have anywhere to run,
I could go and stay in the park,
But it is cold and dark.

I'm not a tramp,
I have a bad cramp,
Everyone stares,
No one even cares,
You treat me badly,
But I can't do anything about it sadly.

Who am I?
I always cry,
I'm always sad,
I'm going mad,
What should I do?
I just need some help.

Thasini Doluweera Watta Gamage (11)
The Sacred Heart Language College, Harrow

THE NIGHT CREATURE CREEPS

The monster crawls in the gloomy darkness,
And waits and waits with eagerness.
Nowhere to be seen in the brightness
He's waiting, just waiting to grab you.

The night lurker peers from under your bed,
Not a noise or sound to be said
They want to eat you for lunch not break instead
Just waiting, just waiting to rip you apart.

The child eating creatures awake in the night,
They don't want your mum to catch them in moonlight.
Shhh... Listen to the child that just got a fright
They're waiting, just waiting to bite your flesh.

The ghosts that rule the moon,
Will be coming for you soon.
So be careful because it's nearly noon.
Oh, he's coming, just coming for... You!

Amanda Tarka (11)
The Sacred Heart Language College, Harrow

MONSTERS

You see them every day
They come and run away
They scare you every night
To make you fly away
Away to your dreams
Where life can begin
This is the story
Of monsters in bed
They come and eat you
To make themselves fed
Once they've eaten
They come to play
But not your game.
You scream and shout
To make them go out.
They stay till midnight
Until your mum goes away
And goes to sleep
In the day, day, day
Thinking that you're OK
When you're stuck
Through night and day
They won't let you go away!

Klaudia Karolina Zajac (11)
The Sacred Heart Language College, Harrow

WINTER WONDERLAND

Snow falling everywhere,
Children playing in the snow,
Icy icicles hanging from roofs,
Joyful people playing games,
The snow is as cold as ice.

Christmas Day comes,
Everyone's opening presents,
They sit around the table,
Eating their meal,
Everyone is happy and joyful spending time together,
Children playing outside,
Stepping on the ice, *crunch, snap*

Icy-cold water everywhere,
The snow has melted *drip, drip,*
Everyone's indoors,
Children playing with their toys.

Brianne Jade Conlon (11)
The Sacred Heart Language College, Harrow

DRIFTING APART

3 years of age, you're friends
If you have a fight you make amends.

11 years of age, you're best friends
You may drift apart,
But never at heart.

The next day you hear a devastating rumour,
But then find out it's all about you.
You're so upset you don't know what to do,
So instead you end up crying in the loo.

You thought everything was going well
But you realised how cruel some people can be
You grow up and move on, find new friends
And don't make amends.

20 years of age, you're enemies
You're drifted apart,
This time at heart.

Izabela Dan (11)
The Sacred Heart Language College, Harrow

DEAD IN THE NEXT 24 HOURS!

Death is the thing underneath the bed that we all fear,
You'd think it's far but it's actually near.
Death is the thing that devours,
People who die every 24 hours.

We all know we're eventually going to die,
So try your hardest in everything, try, try, try.
Thump! Thump! Thump! The sound of Death knocking at your door,
It takes away everything, everything from the top to the core.

Twisting and turning, it works its way to your heart,
Once inside, starts to take everything apart.
You physically and emotionally feel so much pain,
Everything's being taken, all you've worked to gain.

So you come to the end of your earthly travel,
All your great works start to unravel.
You're rid of all your body's powers,
Because you know you will be
Dead in the next 24 hours!

Erica Sagoe (11)
The Sacred Heart Language College, Harrow

I HOPE...

I hope to become a pop star
Touring all over the world.
Driving in my brand new expensive car,
And all of my albums being sold.

I hope to win the lottery,
And be the richest person ever,
To own expensive pottery
And to be that person who tells you, 'never say never'.

I hope to travel the globe,
In private jets and planes,
To own my first golden robe
And to go somewhere where it never rains.

I hope to be an inspiration,
For people to look up to,
To reach my final destination,
And for your hopes to come true.

Kerys Sian Manuel
The Sacred Heart Language College, Harrow

THE SEASIDE DEATH MYSTERY

A cold body is seen through the distance,
Wondering what's happened? They all have persistence.
They walk closer and closer,
Crunch is the sound of the footsteps on the pebbles
They find the dead body, blood swimming into the sea.

Who did it? Who did it? The people chatter,
The body is as wrinkled as fish batter.
They call the police to investigate this incredible crime,
Hundreds and hundreds of people gather around this man
The aggressive adults back their children away from the bloody body.

The little children are scared and crying,
While the hungry crows are flying.
The patient police are trying to identify the killer,
So don't let anyone at the seaside sneak their way home.
Is this day at the seaside ruined after all?

News comes in that there is an eye witness,
The person was apparently full of bitterness.
Was he blending in and wearing normal beach day wear,
Or was he standing out and being the odd one out.
What weapon was used, was it a gun or a knife?

I guess this mysterious crime will remain unsolved.

Kimberley Osayande (11)
The Sacred Heart Language College, Harrow

HAVE YOU?

Have you been in a place
Where it's insecure and unsafe.
No one knows that you're there?
Well, I have.

Have you been in a place scared
And worried that you are unwanted by everyone?
Well, I have.

Have you been in a place
Where you have lost your friends,
And you are being bullied for nothing?
Well, I have.

Take a look,
You know nothing about me.
I'm here to spread my voice.
I'm here for a reason.

I was put here by God,
And I'm staying.
In fact, I think that I'm great.
I have a purpose for being here.

Elizabeth Moran (12)
The Sacred Heart Language College, Harrow

YoungWriters
Est. 1991

YOUNG WRITERS INFORMATION

We hope you have enjoyed reading this book – and that you will continue to in the coming years.

If you're a young writer who enjoys reading and creative writing, or the parent of an enthusiastic poet or story writer, do visit our website www.youngwriters.co.uk. Here you will find free competitions, workshops and games, as well as recommended reads, a poetry glossary and our blog.

If you would like to order further copies of this book, or any of our other titles give us a call or visit **www.youngwriters.co.uk**.

Young Writers
Remus House
Coltsfoot Drive
Peterborough
PE2 9BF

(01733) 890066
info@youngwriters.co.uk